DAISY OSBORN

NEW LIFE
FOR
WOMEN

BOOKS BY
DAISY AND T.L. OSBORN

FIVE CHOICES FOR WOMEN WHO WIN
GOD'S LOVE PLAN
HEALING THE SICK - A Living Classic
HOW TO BE BORN AGAIN
NEW LIFE FOR WOMEN
POWER OF POSITIVE DESIRE
RECEIVE MIRACLE HEALING
SOULWINNING — A Classic on Evangelism
THE BEST OF LIFE
THE GOOD LIFE
THE GOSPEL, ACCORDING TO T.L. & DAISY
THE WOMAN BELIEVER
THERE'S PLENTY FOR YOU
WOMAN WITHOUT LIMITS
WOMEN & SELF-ESTEEM
YOU ARE GOD'S BEST

Most Osborn books and audio or video cassettes are available at quantity discounts for bulk purchases, to be used for gifts, resale, ministry outreaches, educational or other purposes.

For these and other titles, write to:
OSFO PUBLISHERS
P.O. Box 10, Tulsa, OK 74102 USA

Publisher

Australia: Box 54, GPO, Sydney, NSW 2001 (A.R.B.N. 000 419 670)
Canada: Box 281, Adelaide St. Post Sta., Toronto M5C 2J4
England: Box 148, Birmingham B3 2LG (A Registered Charity)

DEDICATED

to

women

who desire

to be

all that God

designed

them

to be.

THE AUTHOR

Bible Quotations in this book have been personalized, and sometimes synopsized, to encourage individual application. They are derived from The New King James Version and the Living Bible unless otherwise noted.

The Author

ISBN 0-87943-089-3

Copyright 1991 by Daisy Washburn Osborn

Printed in the United States of America

All Rights Reserved

CONTENTS

INTRODUCTION

by Pastor LaDonna Osborn*

MY MOTHER, Daisy Marie Washburn was born the tenth of eleven children of California fruit farmers. Her early years were marked by difficulty and poverty. She recounts that her family was so poor, *even the poor folks called us poor!*

At the impressionable age of eight years, Daisy lost her mother and an older sister in a tragic auto/train accident. The children were divided among foster and family homes, to be raised under the distant eye of State welfare agencies. Daisy was raised by an older, married sister who had two children of her own. No stranger to heartache, Daisy lost three more family members before she was out of her teens — two brothers to suicide and her father to murder.

---

*Rev. LaDonna Osborn, daughter of T.L. and Daisy Osborn, is pastor of Int'l Gospel Center, a world missionary church located in Tulsa, Oklahoma, USA.

A born survivor, Daisy blossomed in spite of these compounded circumstances. Seeded by a wise and caring school teacher with this challenge: *You cannot help the way you are born, but you can determine the way you die,* Daisy resolved early to not die in poverty. She set her course to pursue a career in business and finance, excelling in her studies.

Thriving on challenge and competition, Daisy did well in school sports. She mastered the clarinet and proudly played in the marching band. Then she won the honored position of first violinist in her school orchestra.

Recognizing the remarkable ability of this talented young musician, Daisy's instructor, a violinist herself, decided to present Daisy with the dream of a lifetime. She wanted Daisy as her protégée and offered to finance the further education and training that would set Daisy on her way to becoming a professional in the prestigious world of symphonic music.

However, Daisy was as dynamically involved in her church as she was in the public school. When twelve years old, she accepted Jesus Christ as the master and role-model for her life. She was active in youth leadership at fifteen. The scars of earlier heartache and difficulty did not make Daisy a bitter person. To the contrary, she constantly sought out ways to encourage and to lift other people. Her philosophy of life, even at that young age, was to spread only good news about another person.

Never one to sit on the sidelines, Daisy was (and is) an avid volunteer. The seed of a powerful idea was planted in this vivacious young lady when a woman missionary from India visited her church and asked for a volunteer. Daisy found herself on the platform being wrapped in a *sari* — the native dress for the women of India. And before returning to her seat, she heard this life-seeding question, *Would you like to be a missionary when you grow up?*

When presented with her music teacher's *dream of a lifetime,* Daisy was overwhelmed, but she was already carrying in her young heart a dream for her own life — that of becoming a missionary to India. She gently, but forthrightly declined the offer. Her instructor, a wise woman, commended Daisy, and in tears responded: *My dear I think you have made the best choice.*

Daisy's *choice* set her on course to dynamically impact millions of lives, in over 70 nations already. (Be sure to get her powerful book, *5 Choices For Women Who Win*, in which she shares the vital choices she made, which lifted her from mediocrity to excellence.)

When she was sixteen, Daisy met T.L. Osborn, an equally dedicated young man — an evangelist/musician, the twelfth of thirteen children, born of Oklahoma farmers.

Daisy married her handsome "Okie" on Easter Sunday following her seventeenth birthday. It was a new beginning for this courageous young woman and she set out, together with her man, to change her world for good.

Daisy and T.L. were pastoring a church when she was only 19; she was a missionary to India at the age of 20; she was crusading in worldwide mass evangelism at 23, and was the co-founder of a world missionary organization at 24.

During these years Daisy experienced the hoped-for joys of motherhood four times. But the heartbreaks of burying two daughters as infants and her only son as a young adult also invaded her life. Daisy chose to transform those sorrows into strengths for helping other people through their hurts and their heartaches.

Her life has been a series of right choices which have taken her around the world in unequaled Christian service and ministry to multitudes of hurting, needy people of over 70 nations.

Perhaps no woman ever lived who could match Dr. Daisy Osborn's track-record in personal and public preaching and teaching ministry to so many millions of people, face to face, in so many nations, to so many tribes, cultures, races and religions. It is doubtful if any woman ever lived who has witnessed so many healing miracles.

Daisy's prolific ministry of teaching, preaching, writing, recording — plus her organizational abilities, is influencing millions with the message of the gospel — helping women of the world to discover their dignity and their destiny in God's plan of redemption.

Dr. Daisy Washburn Osborn is the Chairperson and a founding Pastor of OSFO International Gospel Center, a World Missionary Church Organization headquartered in Tulsa, Oklahoma, USA. OSFO's eight sister organizations in Australia, Belgium, Canada, England, France, Germany New Zealand and Switzerland are all dedicated to reaching the unreached of the world.

Daisy's natural business acumen has been proven throughout the many years of her multiple responsibilities, administering the vast worldwide soulwinning outreaches of OSFO International and the coordination of all the Osborn Mass-Evangelism Crusades, follow-up Teaching Seminars and National Women's Conferences — besides her full share of preaching to the masses in their crusades.

Dr. Daisy is a Christian humanitarian and a truly international personality, a world citizen, able to speak both French and Spanish, a *diplomate extraordinaire*. Distinguished by unselfish, untiring love-service to people, her path through life is a journey of purposeful connections — with women and men, girls and boys, of all ages, from all lifestyles and philosophies.

Perhaps Daisy is best known for her unconditional dedication to and accomplishments for the betterment of needy people throughout the world community. Skilled in diplomacy and a natural in public relations, she has distinguished experience in dealing with government leaders abroad concerning gospel enterprises.

Jesus has appeared to Daisy personally. Years ago, God spoke to her in an audible voice and called her to *preach the gospel to women.* She looks to God as her source and to Jesus Christ as her role-model — her master. Daisy is a dynamic Jesus-woman giving her life to tell the world: *Jesus Christ is alive! I have seen Him!*

Daisy's public ministry and her writing are interwoven with firsthand experiences that produce a rich and trustworthy document, a guide for self-study and practical growth. They constitute a powerful influence to convince women everywhere to seek the extraordinary purpose that God has for them — to really appropriate God's *New Life For Women.*

Her perceptive teaching motivates true self-development. Her unique style opens new doors in one's thinking that will never close again. The teachings of Jesus become fresh, alive and personal as she walks through the scriptures and points to God's answers for today's questions concerning women.

Daisy motivates women to find within themselves those special gifts and talents which, when linked to God's perfect design, produce the fruits of fulfillment, self-esteem and true happiness.

Because her message is one that applies universally, embracing all ages and lifestyles, Daisy literally influences women around the world to rise from the handicaps of tradition and culture to the reality of God's redemptive dream for all who believe on Jesus Christ, regardless of sex, race or color. She ministers to multitudes and to individuals alike, in the same discerning and healing way.

Here is a woman of consequence, a practical choice maker, who has earned her credentials out in the tough field of action, among people of so many cultures and religions.

Daisy is a pacesetter of courage and commitment — an example of what God can do through a woman who dares to be all that God designed her to be. Her grace, spiritual strength and power provide a model for millions of women and girls seeking guidance in fulfilling their potential for Christ. Her liberating message of Jesus Christ's love and miracle possibilities is setting women and girls around the world free to be all they can be for God through His *New Life*.

Daisy's energetic, humorous, startling and profound styles of communication demonstrate how any woman or girl can be an ingenious and a stout-hearted agent of change in her worlds of influence, boldly following Jesus in a life of rewarding service to others. Her words are rich with the voice of love and experience. Her contribution is gifting the world with a testament of courage and truth.

Daisy's lifetime passion and expertise in lifting people has caused women around the world to discover, from her teachings, their own dynamic potential. She encourages them to actively participate in the Great Commission given by Jesus to all believers.

Since Jesus expresses Himself through the lives of believers — women as well as men, Daisy has demonstrated the faith and the courage to tackle the impossible. Her accomplishments set her apart, and qualify her to help others discover the powerful Jesus-lifestyle. Her message and her example help women discover that in Jesus Christ there is total equality of persons; that every believer shares the same relationship with Christ, the same identity with Him, the same ministry, the same calling, the same anointing — regardless of race, status, color or gender.

In her varied capacities — soulwinner, business executive, preacher, author, teacher, wife, mother, grandmother great-grandmother and world ambassador for Jesus Christ — Dr. Daisy Marie Washburn Osborn is truly one of God's special women for today. Her more than four decades of action in over 70 nations have prepared her for the unique ministry to which God has called her — to preach the gospel to women.

Dr. Daisy is not just speaking nice words. She is in action — doing something that counts to lift the women of the world to their true identity and to their true dignity as Christ's representatives.

Daisy is a woman of faith. She prays and she gets answers. She is a woman believer who never backs down from Satan's threats or lies.

Dr. Daisy knows what a woman is worth in Christ. She knows that redemption is not sexual — that it applies to women as much as it

does to men.   She knows that the power of the
Holy Spirit is no different in a woman than it
is in a man.   She knows that Christ's promises,
His commission and His gifts to the church are
never qualified according to gender — that they
are as effective in and as applicable to a woman believer as they are to a man.

Dr. Daisy knows that God paid the same
price to redeem, to justify and to restore
women to Him as His friends and His partners,
as He paid for men.   She knows that women
who receive Christ can become His witnesses
and His representatives as much as men can.
She knows that Jesus Christ, at work in and
through a woman, is the same as He is at work
in and through a man.

This book is a messenger of good news to
you, helping you to discover your own dignity
and your own destiny in God's plan of redemption.   As you read its pages you are marking
yourself for God's best to come to YOU.   You
are taking a vital step toward discovering the
fullness of His *New Life For Women.*

WOMEN'S NATIONAL CONFERENCE — E. AFRICA

Daisy Osborn seeds the women of the world in her national women's mass rallies abroad.

INDONESIAN WOMEN'S DAY — SURABAYA

WOMEN'S NATIONAL MIRACLE DAY — KAMPALA

AUSTRALIAN CONFERENCE

GOD'S WOMAN
By T.L. Osborn

God's woman
  She has been redeemed;
God's woman
  She has new esteem.

  She's come alive.
  She's on the rise.
  She has a choice
  She has a voice.

God's woman
  With a mission and a call;
God's woman
  With a vision for us all.

  She's anointed. She's a witness
  She's appointed. She is gifted.
  Christ is her identity
  Of dignity and destiny.

The blood of Christ removed her shame.
  Now she acts in Jesus' name.
The power of the Holy Ghost
  Has sent her to the uttermost.

God's woman
  Of faith and hope and power.
God's woman,
  With life and love this hour.

I

WINNING

WITH

CHRIST

TO WIN WITH CHRIST, you applaud, you recognize, you welcome and you release your God-given power to respond to His ability within you.

> *Choose to utilize God's ability*
> *That's within you;*
>
> *And respond to every opportunity*
> *That surrounds you.*

It is not what we have, but how we use it.
It is not what we take, but what we give.
It is not how we pray, but how we live.

Happiness is knowing that you as a woman, are a winner in Christ, by releasing Him for action in and through you.

* Christ thinks through our mind now.

* Christ loves through our heart now.

* Christ helps through our hands now.

* Christ listens through our ears now.

* Christ speaks through our voice now.

Chapter 1

WINNING WITH CHRIST

I WAS IN Lubumbashi, Zaire preparing for our crusade there when I had an unusual experience that prompted me to respond to God's ability in me and to learn the French language.

I was in town for several weeks organizing a mass crusade before my husband, T.L. Osborn, joined me. Each morning about ten o'clock I would take a break and go to a certain sidewalk cafe for a cup of coffee.

There was a businesswoman in town who frequented the cafe about the same time, so we became acquainted.

Rachel was an Italian Jewess, born in South Africa, who spoke seven languages fluently. I was amazed and I could not help but rationalize that she certainly was no smarter than I. And I asked myself: *Then why is it that she speaks SEVEN languages, but I only speak English and Spanish?*.

After we had been meeting for a few days, she asked if I could purchase some clothing for her when I returned to the States. She showed me a catalog that was almost pornographic. I could not understand why she wanted me, a preacher of the gospel, to buy scanty clothes for her.

I said,

Rachel, why do you want these clothes? What is your profession?

She replied,

I am a prostitute.

Well, of course, I was surprised, but thankful that I had sown the seeds of the gospel in her.

But something had happened inside of me.

I went back to my room that day. I got on my knees and I wept. I prayed that God would help me to win Rachel to Him.

Motivation To Learn French

I said to the Lord:

Jesus, Rachel speaks seven languages so that she can market her body in promiscuous and demeaning relationships with men. I have a much more noble and more worthy motive for speaking languages. My reason is to communicate the gospel to the hurting and needy peoples of other nations. I want to be an instrument through which God can channel real *Life For Women*.

I decided — I made the choice to celebrate my responsibility to communicate Jesus to my world. I *did something* about it!

I was impressed to hire a professor and I began to study French. The Lord impressed me: *You apply yourself, then leave the miracle to me.*

Now, both my husband and I preach and teach in three languages — English, Spanish — and French.

What we did was to respond to God's ability within us. That is the way of *Winning With Christ.*

God is the one who originally confused the languages.[1] He can unscramble them to help us to communicate the gospel to people.

Concerning *Winning With Christ,*

FIRST: What do I mean by it?

SECOND: When does one do it?

THIRD: How do we do it?

What Do I Mean?

You will discover the principle of *Winning With Christ* when you choose the positive attitude that you are hooked up with God;

That you are commissioned to *go;*

That you have intelligence to *know;*

That you are entrusted with talents to *grow;* That you are endowed with abilities to *sow;*

That you are a creature of importance to *show* God's goodness to your world.

This is the dynamic, positive attitude of *Winning With Christ.*

My husband wrote a poem that expresses what I mean by *Winning With Christ.*

> *God chose you*
> *So He knows you.*

> *He goes with you*
> *And He glows in you.*

> *He shows that you*
> *Are "pro" and new,*

> *And so, He says*
> *"Bravo!" to you.*

To be a winner with Christ, you applaud, you recognize, you welcome and you release your God-given power to respond to His ability at work in you. I call that responsibility. I believe that is real *Life For Women.*

You go at life with enthusiasm because you are a winner and you know it. You are on God's team. You are valuable. You cannot lose. You experience total happiness.

You believe that *greater is He that is in you than He that is in the world.*[2]

You are thankful that *God always causes you to triumph.*[3]

You rejoice because you know that *in all things you are more than a conqueror through Christ who loves you.*[4]

You celebrate the fact that you and God can do anything. You accept responsibility for your part in this teamwork by your response to God's ability in you. You succeed. You are fulfilled. You discover the real principle of *Winning With Christ.*

When Do We Respond?

FIRST: When do we apply this principle of *Winning With Christ?*

Every time we have an opportunity to respond to God's ability within us.

> *An opportunity not hasted*
> *Is ability that is wasted.*

> *And ability that is unused*
> *Is talent that is abused.*

You are the only one who can utilize your own ability. That fact provides wonderful security for you because, what you have is yours to do with as you choose.

> *Choose to utilize God's*
> *ability*
> *That's within you;*

> *And respond to every*
> *opportunity*
> *That surrounds you.*

Life For Women is realized in its fullness when you discover that people are your greatest opportunity, that whenever you encounter people in need, you have found a field to seed.

So you apply this principle of *Winning With Christ* every time you meet a human person in need and respond to that need with God's ability within you.

The classic principle for winning in life is still:

Find a need and meet it.

Find a hurt and heal it.

When you practice doing that, you discover real *Life For Women.* God's ability responds through you as a woman, to meet human needs and to heal human hurts. You are practicing the principle of *Winning With Christ.*

How Do We Do It?

How do we apply this principle of *Winning With Christ?*

By our power of choice.

Instead of looking at the world in need around us and instead of complaining about human misery and suffering, we choose to practice the awareness of Christ's mission functioning through us.

We are here as His teammates to meet human needs, to give solutions where there are problems, to give strength where there is weakness, to bring joy and happiness where there is grief and sorrow.

St. Francis of Assisi prayed:

> *Lord, make me an instrument of peace.*
>
> *Where there is hatred, let me sow love;*
>
> *Where there is injury, let me sow pardon;*
>
> *Where there is doubt, let me sow faith;*
>
> *Where there is despair, let me sow hope;*
>
> *Where there is darkness, let me sow light;*
>
> *Where there is sadness, let me sow joy.*

St. Francis had discovered the principle of *Winning With Christ*.

Worship Or Service

It seems to me that the most alluring seduction in religion is to be engrossed in worship instead of being involved in service.

We discover the principle of *Winning With Christ* when we discover these facts:

* Christ thinks through our mind now.

* Christ loves through our heart now.

* Christ helps through our hands now.

* Christ listens through our ears now.

* Christ speaks through our voice now.

When I respond to Christ's ability in me to make people happier and to make my world better, I am a winner — I have learned the principle of *Winning With Christ* — I have discovered real *Life For Women.*

The Jesus Principle

True happiness for yourself comes in seeking to give true happiness to others. It is the principle of sowing and reaping.

Everyone desires happiness.

Why is it that so many who earnestly seek happiness actually create for themselves a hell on earth?

If you seek happiness for yourself and ignore the needs of people around you, you find
only misery, exasperation, irritation and dissat-
isfaction.

The Jesus-principle of winning is reaching
out to lift and to help someone else, to look for
others who have burdens and to share them.

>To observe the problems of
>people and to solve them.

>To perceive the hurts of hu-
>man persons and to heal them.

*Blessed are the merciful, for they shall obtain
mercy.*[5]   That is the way you create heaven on
earth instead of hell on earth.

Mother Teresa said: *We all long for heaven,
where God is. But we have it in our power to be
in heaven with God right now ... by loving the
unlovely as He does, by helping the helpless as
He does, by giving to those in need as He does,
by serving the lonely as He serves, by rescuing
the perishing as He rescues. This is my Christ.
This is the way I live.*

The Real Thing

Malcolm Muggeridge, the renowned British
news analyst went to Calcutta to see the beautiful love-ministry of Mother Teresa.

Talking with her, Dr. Muggeridge said that
he was amazed by the happiness of the sisters

who made up her team and he asked her, *Is it genuine? Or is it a pretension?*

Mother Teresa replied: *No, my friend, it is not a pretense. You see, nothing makes a person so happy as to really reach out in mercy to someone who is hurting, and to help them in some way.*

The best prescription for winning, for happiness and for a life of joy is to imitate the Jesus-way: *Do to others as you would have them do to you.*[6]

Reaching out to others has its recompense built into its deed. The harvest is in the seed. The act of love prophesies its own benediction. The future reward is part and parcel of the present act.

Faith combined with actions of good for others, is the way that Christ can come alive in you as a woman.

The missionary doctor in the African bush who was asked why he was willing to perform surgery in places where he could hope for no monetary recompense answered: *It makes me feel so good inside knowing that my hands, for a few hours, have been the hands of Jesus Christ healing the sick.* His surgical procedures are *celebrations* for him.

How do you and I apply this principle of *Winning With Christ?*

Instead of complaining about problems, we recognize that without them there would be no need for solutions, no need to probe, to think, to learn, or to discover.

Instead of lamenting human misery, we take action that relieves suffering. We contemplate the gladness and the delight that fills human lives when remedies are discovered.

We realize that without the night, there would be no morning; that springtime follows the cold winter; that clouds enhance the rainbow.

Release The Power Within You

So that is how you apply this principle of *Winning With Christ.* As a woman with real life in you, you liberate your God-given talents, your gifts, your power of choice to reach out to serve, to bless, to heal and to lift your world.

You see yourself as a team-mate with Christ among people and you comprehend that living is giving. That is the ultimate of *Life For Women.*

Elbert Hubbard said, *Down in their hearts, wise persons know this truth: The only way to help yourself is to help others.*

George Bernard Shaw said: *A thinking person is one who puts more into life than they take out.*

Mother Teresa said:

If sometimes poor people have had to die of starvation, it is not because God didn't care for them, but because you and I didn't give, were not instruments of love in the hands of God, to give them that bread, to give them that clothing, because we did not recognize Him, when once more Christ came in distressing disguise   in the hungry person, in the lonely person, in the homeless child, and seeking for shelter.

Christ has identified Himself with the hungry, the sick, the naked, the homeless; hunger, not only for bread, but for love, for care, to be somebody to someone; nakedness, not of clothing only, but nakedness of that compassion that very few give to the unknown; homelessness, not only just for a shelter made of stone, but that homelessness that comes from having no one to call your own.

Today Christ is in the people who are unwanted, unemployed, uncared for, hungry, naked and homeless. It is you and I as Christians who must find them, and help them ... Thoughtfulness is the beginning of great sanctity.   Jesus went about doing good.

A Christian is a tabernacle of the living God. He created me, He chose me, He came to dwell in me, because He wanted me ... It is natural that you spend the rest of your life radiating Christ's love.

Knowing that Christ dwells in you with His unlimited power and His unconditional love at work through you, is happiness in itself. For a woman, that is truly *Winning With Christ.*

You perceive that you are a people-person, a messenger, an example, a walking, living embodiment of Jesus in the flesh, touching and helping people.

General William Booth of the Salvation Army said, *Before you can change society, you must change people — individually. No matter how many degrees you may have, at the bottom of it all is people contacting people, one at a time, and effecting a change for the better in their lives.*

In response to all He has done for us , let us outdo each other in being helpful and kind to each other and in doing good.[7]

Life is a sacred trust.

> *It's not what we have,*
>> *but how we use it.*

> *It's not what we take,*
>> *but what we give.*

> *It's not how we pray,*
>> *but how we live.*

Touch People — Touch Christ

Remember the words of Christ: *I was hungry and you fed me, I was naked and you clothed me, I was thirsty and you gave me to drink, I was sick and in prison and you visited me.*[8]

You comprehend that your life's purpose is PEOPLE. And you understand that God is at work in you as a woman, reaching people through your hands, through your love, through your life.

That is applying the true principle of *Winning With Christ*. You choose to respond to God's ability inside you, to minister to the people of your world all around you.

You do it because you have faith in Jesus who is at work in you.

A remarkable inscription marks a certain tomb in Saint Paul's Cathedral at London. It reads:

Sacred to the memory of ---, who at all times and everywhere gave strength to the weak, substance to the poor, sympathy to the suffering, all as devotion to God.

The highest possible worship of God is our service to human persons.

Jesus said: *If you have faith as a grain of mustard seed you shall say to this mountain move from here and it will move. Nothing shall be impossible to you.*[9]

The Bible says, *With God* in you *nothing shall be impossible.*[10] Be sure that you add the *in you.*

We do not sit back and wait for God to do all of the work. He has put His ability in you and in me. He has given you and me the power of His Holy Spirit to do the job.

You Can Do Anything

Celebrate the world of need
  That surrounds you,

By activating the Holy Spirit
  That is within you,

To communicate the Jesus
  Who saves you.

Which produces the happiness
  That thrills you.

With the Holy Spirit of God in you, you as a woman can do anything, and that is happiness. That is *Winning With Christ.* That is authentic *Life For Women.*

Ordinary people celebrate
  their achievements.

But the winners celebrate
  their responsibilities.

My husband, T.L. Osborn says:

GOD IS SPIRIT!

WE ARE HIS FLESH!

We are God's expressions on this earth now. We are His body — His hands, His feet, His voice.

Winning With Christ is knowing that nothing is impossible for you and Him as a team.

You can choose to win with Christ by choosing to act in His name. Whether you choose to be a clerk (who waits for a customer) or a salesperson (who goes out and finds a customer) is up to you. You can choose to ring doorbells instead of church bells; to reach out and to bless people in proximity instead of by proxy; to win by person instead of by purse.

Happiness for a woman is knowing that you are a winner in Christ by releasing Him for action in you.

Jesus said to both women and men:

I give you power ... over all the power of the enemy and nothing shall by any means hurt you.[11]

Remember, God's *power* is given to make us servants to humanity.

The Living Bible says:

I can do everything that God asks me to do, with the help of Christ who gives me the strength and the power.[12]

Nine Winning Principles

Here are nine valuable guiding principles in *Winning With Christ.*

1. *Practice* the art of doing for others what you want them to do for you.

2. *Recognize* and value the unique person that you are.

3. *Accept* responsibility for the fact that your life is and will always be what you yourself make of it through your innate powers of choice, of decision and of action.

4. *Absorb* the concept that failure is never final, so if you do not succeed the first time, keep on trying.

5. *Realize* that whatever is worth your doing is worth doing the very best that you can.

6. *Understand* that true happiness is having hope, experiencing love and doing things for the betterment of people.

7. *Assimilate* the irreversible law that you are, and that you become the tangible reality of the sum and substance of your own thoughts.

8. *Grasp* the winning criterion that what you learn, discover, prove and know becomes the only power that you yourself can utilize in this world.

9. *Actualize* the power within you by being calm and confident, accepting your own uniqueness, by knowing your distinct purpose, by being sure that your goals are right and good for God, for people and for yourself; and by going forward with Him as your source, without intimidation, inferiority or hesitation.

The Winner's Celebration

When you assimilate these nine guiding principles, you can know the true happiness of *Winning With Christ.*

Bible References:

1. Ge.11:6-7
2. Jn.4:4
3. 2Co.2:14
4. Ro.8:37
5. Mt.5:7
6. Lu.6:31
7. He.10:24 LB
8. Mt.25:35-36
9. Mt.17:20
10. Lu.1:37
11. Lu.10:19
12. Ph.4:13 LB

Dr. Daisy believes a successful teacher is an avid student. She says, "No one learns everything, but everyone can learn something. Once you have knowledge then you can impart it to someone else.

Daisy Osborn's private library contains rare treasures of knowledge to help womankind achieve the dignity of success.

II

CHOICES

FOR

WINNERS

SOCIETY'S cultural attitude hardly identifies a woman except through a man. That tradition causes many women to forget their individuality, their unique abilities, their power of choice, and their right to achieve greatness.

You are God's idea in human form.

This book will help you to launch your personal treasure hunt, to discover your innate abilities, talents and skills.

Let no voice or influence:

   * Prevent your fulfillment.

   * Retard your happiness.

   * Impede your creativity.

   * Stunt your effectiveness.

   * Frustrate your objectives.

Learn four virtues and five *Choices For Winners.*

Chapter 2

CHOICES FOR WINNERS

EVERY WOMAN can be a winner. You were destined to win. You are not a loser, but a chooser. You can actually choose to win.

I am going to show you how to do that.

I want to ask you some questions to help you absorb the valuable input God has destined to come to you through this book.

The fact that you are reading this book right now indicates that God has chosen you to be one of the happy successful women on His team for life.

1. Do you realize that you are a unique individual?

2. Did you know that there is not another person in the whole world like you?

3. Are you aware that God made you special, just the way He wants you, with a unique purpose?

4. Do you accept the fact that you were born with an abundance of ability?

5. Are you aware that God's plan for your life requires talent, ability and skill?

6. Do you embrace the reality that those gifts are already in you?

7. Do you practice the awareness that you are extraordinary because you are one-of-a-kind?

8. Do you value the fact that you are bestowed with all of the talents you will ever need in your whole life?

9. Do you know that in discovering your inner response to your God-given abilities, you as a woman, can be only one thing — a winner?

When you have even a little self-love and self-worth — because of your awareness of God in you — you will start developing Christ-motivated habits that will make you a winner for sure.

The Awesome Preview

There are only two categories of people:

  *The losers and the choosers.

  *The whiners and the shiners.

  *Those who reject ability and those who respond to ability.

  *The doers and the non-doers.

  *The believers and the unbelievers.

This fact is vividly portrayed in the preview which Christ gave us of the day when we shall all stand before the King to give an account of what we have done, or have not done, for Him during our life.[1]

There is just one division:

The doers are separated from the non-doers.

Race is not a factor, neither is our skin color, our social status, our culture, our language or our sex.

The division is based on action and non-action. The action involves things that are very basic — very simple.

The verses to which I am referring talk about such things as feeding the hungry, visiting the prisoners, clothing the naked.

Anyone Can Do It

Could not just about anyone give bread to the hungry, or water to the thirsty, or housing to a stranger, or clothing to the naked, or a helping hand to someone sick, or make a friendly call on a prisoner?

No special ability is required. Only God's ability to love, to care, to comfort and to share.

An awareness of, and an act of meeting a human need is all that is expected. Nothing big.

Something everyone can do. But the DOING is what counts.

Here are the words of our Lord in Matthew 25. Just notice how basic they are:

The Doers — The Non-Doers

When I shall come in my glory, then I shall sit upon my throne. And all the nations shall be gathered before me. I will separate the people as a shepherd separates the sheep from the goats, and place the sheep at my right hand, and the goats at my left.

Then I shall say to those at my right, 'Come, blessed of my Father, into the Kingdom prepared for you from the founding of the world. For I was hungry and you fed me; I was thirsty and you gave me water; I was a stranger and you invited me into your homes; naked and you clothed me; sick and in prison, and you visited me.'

Then these righteous ones will reply, 'Sir, when did we ever see you hungry and feed you? Or thirsty and give you anything to drink? Or a stranger, and help you? Or naked, and clothe you? When did we ever see you sick or in prison, and visit you?'

And I will tell them, 'When you did it to these my sisters and my brothers you were doing it to me!'

Then I will turn to those on my left and say, 'I was hungry and you wouldn't feed me; thirsty, and you wouldn't give me anything to drink; a stranger, and you refused me hospitality; naked, and you wouldn't clothe me; sick and in prison, and you didn't visit me.'

Then they will reply, 'Lord, when did we ever see you hungry or thirsty or a stranger or naked or sick or in prison, and not help you?'

And I will answer, 'When you refused to help the least of these my sisters and my brothers, you were refusing help to me.'

And they shall go away into eternal punishment; but the righteous into everlasting life.[2]

The Overlooked Verse

There is another Bible verse which adds significance to this message.

This verse emphasizes something that many women have overlooked, because of society's cultural attitude that women are hardly identified, except through a man.   That one tradition causes many women to forget their vital role, as an individual, in this life.

We are each one talented, and each of us must account for those talents individually.

Here is that important Bible verse:

Yes, each of us will give an account of herself or of himself to God.[3]

Launch Your Treasure Hunt

I am a good news messenger. Although the scriptures I have cited are weighty, they are not intended to frighten you. They constitute some of the best news you will ever receive.

As you read this message of hope and of courage, you are going to receive some exciting and some creative ideas about your involvement as a Jesus-person, as a soulwinner, as a believer, as a representative of Jesus Christ in your world of influence.

Remember, you are not a loser, but a chooser. You have the power of choice. You have the right to achieve greatness in every area of your life. That is basic to *Life For Women*.

New Awareness

See yourself as you really are. Awaken yourself to a new awareness of your true identity.

When you were conceived in your mother's womb, you were an idea of God taking on human form. You were created special, and God has a distinct purpose — an unparalleled plan for your life.

My goal is to help you to launch your personal treasure hunt. In other words, start from this very moment to discover the innate and the unique abilities which God has created in you to guarantee your fulfillment and your happiness in *Life For Women*.

Perhaps you have never thought of yourself as a gifted person. Well, now is the time to adjust your attitude and to accept God's inventory of the treasures, the talents, the skills and the abilities that He has assigned to you from the moment you were conceived.

You are already bestowed with all of the talents you will ever need in your life. In fact, you have more abilities than you can ever use.

Choosing The Positive

Would you like to learn how to respond to your God-given capabilities? Would you like, once and for all, to discard the frustrating excuses that have prevented your fulfillment as a woman?

Do you want to be rid of negative thoughts that have retarded the winning life you were destined for?

Would you be willing to make a big bold choice today? Would you as a woman, choose to abandon the habits which have impeded your creative usefulness, which have stunted your effective involvement in life, which have frustrated your goals?

As you discover your inner response to your God-given abilities, you will discover that petty excuses will be changed into purposeful uses.

You will observe that negative thoughts will be replaced with positive ideas which will result in happiness for you and for those around you.

You will recognize that non-productive habits will be gone. In their place, your creative talents will be cultivated and channeled for achievement. You will become a true-blue winner, walking in God's new kind of *Life For Women.*

As that takes place in you, you will find yourself looking for a reason to scale and to climb rather than for an excuse to fail and to whine.

Decide today to assure yourself of a life of personal fulfillment, of inner happiness, and of consistent success. Turn those old worn-out excuses into brand-new uses. That is the choice of a winner.

Winners On God's Team

When you as a woman, become aware of Christ in you, you begin developing habits that make you an achiever in His *New Life For Women.*

I was in an African city, preaching and preparing for one of our national crusades. This is always a very busy time and it is easy to get so caught up with high-level meetings that individuals are overlooked. On that particular day, I was meeting the governor of the state, then the mayor of the city and finally the chief of police. It was a very arduous day.

In the course of conversation as we traveled to my first engagement, I heard about Esther, the daughter of a high court judge. She was in the hospital in a coma and was dying.

The judge had heard of my presence in the city and had sought me out. He caught up with our party and appealed to me to come and to minister to his beautiful, young daughter.

A tumor on the brain had caused Esther's sudden collapse at the university where she was an honor student. Her father was heartbroken. So many dreams had seemingly ended in disaster.

The executives of the crusade committee began making excuses for me to the judge. They assured him that I would like to agree to his request but that I had no time.

However, as I heard the plea of the judge and the excuses of the pastors, I seemed to hear Jesus say: "Remember how my well-intentioned disciples tried to stop the cry of Bartimaeus? Follow my example."

That was all I needed to hear.

I interrupted, *Let's go to our next engagement by way of the hospital.* That is what we did.

As the judge and I walked into the room, Esther was lying still as death with her eyes closed. The attending physician confirmed what the justice had told us, *Esther is dying.*

We asked permission to be with her alone and then I took Esther's hand. I did not see my hand on her. I saw the hand of Jesus. I talked to Esther, then prayed and commanded her to open her eyes, in the name of Jesus. Her eye-

lids flickered and then she opened her eyes
wide. A big beautiful smile spread across her
face. She looked angelic! That was the beginning of a great miracle.

Esther was completely restored to health, to
the amazement of many. She attended the crusade and gave witness of her miracle to a field
of over 200,000 people.

Jesus was never too busy, too famous, too
tired or too scheduled to hear a single voice of
a person in need. Jesus in you and in me has
not changed. He is the same today in us.

Christ said we would find Him among the
poor, the naked, the hungry, the thirsty, the sick
and the prisoners.

He emphasized that those who do something
to reach out to bless those kinds of people are
the sure winners on His team; and those who do
nothing about them end up as the unfulfilled
losers in life.

The good news is that today you can choose
to be a winner with Him. You can choose His
brand new and dynamite *Life For Women.*

Only Two Categories

There are only two categories of people
who will stand before our Lord when He makes
the final separation between those who shall be
eternally blessed and those who shall be eternally lost. The doers; the non-doers.

Those who will win in that day, will win because they will have done such simple things — not extraordinary things, but ordinary things to help ordinary, needy people.

Anyone can give bread to the hungry or give water to the thirsty.

Anyone can host a stranger or clothe someone who is naked.

Anyone can lend a helping hand to a sick person or go and visit a prisoner.

Yet, why was it that only the *righteous* ones — the winners, did those things?

Those simple acts of kindness are what distinguished them before the Lord. Those deeds marked them as winners on His team.

They possessed God's ability to love, to care, to comfort, to lift, to reach, to bless, to give, to help and to share.

They had been awakened for winning. And that is happening to you as you read this book. All of the God-given creativity, talent, ability and potentiality which He built into you is coming to life — you are waking up to win with Him. You as a woman, are discovering creative and productive *Life For Women* and how to channel that life into successful living. You are choosing to win through Christ at work in you.

Four Great Virtues

A woman on the winning team with Jesus has at least four wonderful virtues — and you are equipped with these gifts as much as anyone else in the world, once you choose to make your own individual life count with God.

First Virtue: A constant awareness of human need;

Second Virtue: An abiding motivation to meet that need;

Third Virtue: The spontaneous energy to get involved;

Fourth Virtue: The quiet patience to be non-critical.

My Personal Answer

Between our mass crusades abroad, I minister and preach as often as possible in women's conferences, national conventions, training seminars, rallies, etc. God has placed a deep concern and compassion in my heart to help both women and men to become winners in life.

Recently I was the principal speaker at an international conference of more than ten thousand Christian women.

Between lectures, in some *tête-à-tête* discussions, an influential Christian lady strongly objected to my urging women to accept the com-

mand of Jesus to *go to all the world and to
preach the gospel to every creature.*[4]

That lady also strongly objected to me applying Acts 1:8 to women: *You shall receive
power after that the Holy Spirit is come upon
you, and you shall be my witnesses in all the
world.*[5]

She Thought Her Man
Would Answer For Her

She had assumed the traditionally theological
philosophy that women were excluded from
Christ's commission; she had accepted the religious presumption that women were generally
excused from the job of soulwinning.

She said with profound conviction:

*My going and my doing depends entirely
upon my husband. If he doesn't direct me to go
witness for Christ, I don't. He hasn't, so I
haven't.*

I asked her:

*Will your husband answer for you when you
stand before Christ, the King, to account for what
you have done, or not done, during your lifetime?*

*Do you think that we, as women, will be ex-
empted from standing before our Master and
from answering for our own lives?*

She replied, with a searching look in her
eyes:

I really don't know what you are talking about.

I proceeded to relate to her my own personal experience.

My Record Is Personal

One day while reading my Bible these scriptures which I have shared with you stood out forcibly to me.

I was reading Romans Chapter 14, in my Living Bible, which says:

Remember, each of us will stand personally before the Judgment Seat of God. Yes, each of us will give an account of herself or of himself to God.[6]

I realized that I had discovered some declarations in the Bible which, by normal church culture and by ecclesiastical tradition, are overlooked by women.

I had read these verses many times, but that day I discovered the seeds of truth that would have a profound and an eternal effect upon my life — and ultimately on the lives of women around the world.

I realized that one day, I, Daisy Marie Washburn Osborn, will be one of those persons gathered before the King.

What I do, or do not do for people and for my Lord in this life, will determine my classification forever.

T.L. Osborn, my dedicated, soulwinning husband will not answer for me. I will stand alone before the King as an individual. My husband's deeds will not make points for me. My record will stand on its own. I have an individual responsibility, and so do you. I accept it gladly. How about you?

You are important to God. Only you can do the things God has equipped you to do.

It is important to recognize that with God-given ability comes responsibility which is simply this: Your *response* to God's *ability*.

When you realize this, you are on your way to becoming a winner. You are experiencing what it means to discover real *Life For Women*.

Five Positive Choices

I am going to share with you five positive and dynamic choices which you have the freedom to make in your own life. (These are expounded in my book *Five Choices For Women Who Win*.)

These five basic choices can transform any person into a lifetime winner. They can rejuvenate and revitalize you as a woman, right now while you are reading this message.

Choice No. 1.

INDIVIDUALIZE YOURSELF

Choice No. 2.

CELEBRATE YOUR RESPONSIBILITY

Choice No. 3.

BELIEVE YOU CAN RE-BEGIN

Choice No. 4.

IDENTIFY JESUS IN PEOPLE

Choice No. 5.

EXTERMINATE THE EXCUSE SYNDROME

These choices for becoming a winner are really quite simple and they offer formidable options to you for real satisfaction and achievement in *Life For Women*.

They will awaken everything that God has built into you for the purpose of winning in life with Him.

Right now, stop and make this commitment to Christ. Say:

DEAR LORD, I am aware that I shall stand before you and answer for my own life. Thank You for giving me the right to choose to be a woman winner. I choose to do the simple, ordinary things you have placed me here to do.

I recognize my individual uniqueness — that I am special in Your plan.

I celebrate my response to Your ability in me to lift and to help people.

Whatever my past, I do this day choose to re-begin as a winner with You.

I have learned that whatever I say or do to needy people, I say or do to You, Lord.

I resolve to exterminate every excuse for failure. I place my hand in Yours, and I recognize my destiny as a woman is to be your representative on this earth.

My life is Yours. Your life is mine. Together, we can only be winners. I thank You, in Jesus' name for leading me to discover some of the principles of real resourceful and creative *Life For Women*.

AMEN!

Bible References:

1. Ro.14:12
2. Mt.25:31-46
3. Ro.14:12 LB
4. Mk.16:15
5. Ac.1:8
6. Ro.14:10,12

Dr. Daisy clears shipment of tons of gospel literature at national border. After dedication prayer, (left), she distributes it all to church leaders, then gives special encouragement to the women.

III

THE

VALUE OF

PEOPLE

IF YOU AS A WOMAN, are ever tempted to question your value to God, remember what Jesus Christ paid to redeem you.

When you accept your own value, then you can accept God's value of others.

Every miracle God does is proof of *The Value Of People.* My husband, T.L. Osborn, and I may have seen more miracles — during four decades of ministry in over 70 nations — than any couple who ever lived. God's No. 1 business is lifting and blessing people.

Discover your value — to God, to people, and to yourself; then no one can ever make you feel inferior or unloved again.

As a woman, when you discover the principle of your value to God and of His intense love for you, then you can become His co-worker and witness, helping others to discover this marvelous new life.

Chapter 3

THE VALUE OF PEOPLE

THE GREATEST DISCOVERY a woman can make, in order to give meaning and significance to her life, is to realize how much God values her, needs her, and desires that she be His friend and partner in life.

I have personalized these scriptures from the Bible, for you — as a woman. The secret of real faith is to put yourself at the heart of God's promises. Read these verses as I have applied them to you.

For God has rescued you out of the darkness and gloom of Satan's kingdom and brought you into the kingdom of His dear Son, who bought your freedom with His blood and forgave you all your sins.[1]

It was through what Jesus Christ did that God cleared a path for you to come to Him ... for His death on the cross has made peace with God for you by His blood.

This includes you who were once so far away from God. You were His enemies and hated Him and were separated from Him by your evil thoughts and actions, yet now He has brought you back as His friends.

He has done this through the death on the cross of His own human body, and now as a result Christ has brought you into the very presence of God, and you are standing there before Him with nothing left against you ... the only condition being that you fully believe the Truth ... convinced of the Good News that Jesus died for you, and never shifting from trusting Him to save you.

This is the wonderful news that came to you and is now spreading all over the world. And I have the joy of telling it to others.[2]

These verses reveal *The Value Of People.* They reveal your worth as a woman. If you are ever tempted to question your value to God, remember what Jesus Christ paid to redeem you and to restore you to Him. Would He have paid such a price for you if you were not infinitely valuable to him?

Energizing Power

An insane man by the name of Kariuki was brought to one of our mass crusades overseas. Many thousands of people were there.

Kariuki was known as the running maniac. His hair and beard were long, disheveled and flea-infested. His body was filthy. His rags barely covered his nakedness.

He ran across the hills of Kikuyuland for 17 years, practically nude, demented, clutching rubbish in his arms, running from one village to another, throwing the worthless stuff down and desperately gathering more bits and pieces, as though he must cling to something.

God never created anybody to be unable to think and act normally, or to live in shame and disgrace.

A young Christian had reached out to Kariuki in the kind of love that motivates a person to share Christ with others. He conceived a way to entice him into his vehicle so he could bring him to the crusade.

I did not know, nor did my husband, T.L. Osborn, know, that such an insane man was in the audience that day as we preached the gospel and planted the seeds of human value in the minds of the people.

The Miracle Power Of Truth

There is a miraculous power in truth. As a woman, I have learned that words are seeds. They have the ability to produce what they say. They are energizers.

I believe that God's words are energized by His own divine, miracle-working life. He created the world by the power of His word, and the Bible says, *the word of the Lord endures forever.*[3] His word is as powerful today when we speak or teach or announce it, as it ever was. That is what I believe when I stand before the multitudes to teach the powerful and positive gospel of Jesus Christ. That is the secret to

the thousands of miracles which have been witnessed in our crusade meetings.

The day Kariuki was brought to our crusade
in Nyeri, Kenya, we were teaching the people
about being created in God's image, about His
original design and plan for each human being,
about His love for us even though we had sinned, about the price Jesus Christ paid to redeem
us to God, about how to believe the gospel and
to accept Jesus as Savior.

We emphasized the value of each human
person as we ministered that day.

We taught the multitude:

*Each one of you is beautifully and wonder-
fully made in God's image. Every individual
among you is special. You do not have to be second class. You are each unique. God who created
you like Himself, put you here for a purpose so
special that no one else on earth can do what you
are here to do.*

Those word-seeds had power.

There is a remarkable statement in the
Bible about the power of Jesus' words:

*As He was teaching, the power of the Lord
was there to heal the people.*[4]

That has to be what happened to Kariuki
who was brought to our meeting that day.

Everybody Is A Real Somebody

We taught that crowd the essence of what I am sharing with you in this vital book for women. We emphasized that God made no one for failure, poverty, sickness or shame; that everybody is a real *somebody* in God's eyes.

We urged that audience to personally accept the fact that each of them was a special creation of God and to begin believing that by cooperating with God, any person could discover new life through believing on Jesus Christ and through accepting Him by faith.

In some miraculous way those powerful seeds of truth penetrated Kariuki, and his mind was healed and his life was transformed in one glorious moment when God's loving compassion and power restored him to his right mind by a miracle.

The Healing Power
Of God's Word

Almost all of the great miracles that we have witnessed during over four decades of mass evangelism in more than 70 nations — and we may have seen as many or more than any couple has ever been privileged to witness — almost all of them have taken place out in the crowd, while we were teaching the people or praying for them, without us knowing anything about the case until the miracle had already taken place.

Kariuki was out there listening that day as we preached and prayed. The Spirit of the Lord that bathed that great field of people in His love had come upon Kariuki in some way that I cannot explain. In a moment, the demons were gone from him. He was well. He was normal.

He asked the man who brought him, *What am I doing with this stuff in my arms?*

The young Christian realized that Kariuki was really healed. He brought him to the platform so the audience could know about the wonder God had done.

There Kariuki stood. His clothes were so torn and dirty that they scarcely covered his nudity. He looked wild. His hair was long, matted and full of fleas. His beard was long. His body emitted a terrible odor.

But when we looked into his eyes, we could see that this man had been visited by the Lord.

T.L., my husband, took him by the shoulders and said to him, *Kariuki, you look beautiful.* Everybody applauded.

Good Seeds
Grow Good Crops

Then T.L. said, *Kariuki, you are my brother. Did you know that my father and your father is the same? We are one.* And we embraced him in love. The crowd was amazed.

I said to the poor man, *Kariuki, we are so proud of you. You are going to go places. God our father made you. He has a plan for you that nobody in the world can carry out as good as you can.* Then we embraced him again.

Then he gave a beautiful testimony about the horror of his 17 years as a demented maniac, of how Jesus came to him and healed him while we were teaching the gospel, and of how wonderful and peaceful it was to be free from that terrible mental oppression that had destroyed his life for so many years.

When he had finished talking, we asked the local preachers to take him and to help him get a bath and a haircut. Also, they were to buy him new shoes and new clothes, with a beautiful necktie — and to get him a Bible. Then we asked them to bring him back the next day so the multitude could see what God had done.

The next day, Kariuki was seated on the platform. You would have thought he was one of the preachers. In fact, from that day, he continued to sit on the platform during each meeting. He never missed a service.

Every evening, either T.L. or I asked Kariuki to read the scripture lesson before we began to teach. As he read the scriptures the entire community would marvel again at the miracle God had done in their city. Everyone knew Kariuki as the crazy, running maniac. Now they were overwhelmed as they saw him, each day, sane, normal and happy.

Kariuki wore his new suit each day, attending every meeting, listening, learning and developing into a remarkably balanced gentleman.

Kariuki is a classic example of *The Value Of People.*

In Bible days, *many believed on His name, when they saw the miracles which He did.*[5] *And a great multitude followed Him, because they saw the miracles which He did on them that were diseased.*[6]

It was the same in Nyeri. Thousands turned to the Lord because they saw the wonderful miracles which Christ did through the power of the gospel.

Start Your Own Miracle Now

The power of the truths I am sharing with you in this book, brought Kariuki all the way from a running, half naked, wild man to a groomed, well dressed Christian gentleman. He found good employment and has become a positive influence in the Kikuyu community. His is a living example of one who rose from emptiness to meaningful living and discovered his own personal **value** as a marvelous creation of God.

You Are Valuable As You Are

A drunkard, lying in a gutter clutching his bottle, was attracted by a Christian who was sharing the gospel on the street.

The preacher emphasized the importance of life and was trying to help the people to realize their individual value as persons created in God's likeness.

He stressed the price that God had paid for the salvation of each human person; that He loved us so much that He paid for our redemption by giving His own Son, Jesus Christ, to die in our place.

The drunkard was touched by the idea that God valued him that much. It had never occurred to him that his life had value to God.

God Values People As They Are

When the street preacher concluded his talk, the drunk man called out: *Sir, I want to be saved. But I am drunk. I am no good.*

The preacher said, *Friend, God loves you like you are. He created you like Himself. He has already paid to redeem you. He holds nothing against you if you believe Jesus Christ died in your place. He values you just as you are. He has paid for your salvation. Just accept Him and His love for you.*

I do. I do, the drunk man said in tears.

And he was transformed.

In his drunken state, Jesus came to his life and saved and changed him. His bottle had no more appeal. He became a follower of Christ and was restored to a productive life — another vivid proof of *The Value Of People.*

See Yourself As God Sees You

The miracle began when he realized that he was valuable to God.

When you, as a woman, accept your own self-value, you can begin to discover real *Life For Women.* Than you can accept God's value of others and you can begin to share that life with them.

When you realize how God esteems you, how He created you in His own image, then you can accept the fact that YOU, as one of God's offspring, deserve happiness, peace, success and fulfillment in life.

Nobody on earth can ever make you feel inferior, unworthy or undeserving again.

"The Drinks Are On Me"

A personal friend of ours who is the pastor of a large, soulwinning church, was converted and called to preach the gospel while drinking at a bar in a nightclub.

He was thinking about God's love for him and how God valued him just like he was. God's Spirit suddenly visited him as he was standing at the bar. He decided to stop destroying what God had paid so much to save.

He bowed his head and prayed, confessing his sins and accepted Jesus Christ and His love right there in the nightclub.

Leaning on the bar, he wept aloud and received Jesus as His Lord. As he wept, he told the Lord he would give his life to tell others about His love and miracle power.

Then he raised his head, and when he did, he said that dingy nightclub looked like a bit of heaven to him.

His joy and peace were so intense that he wanted to celebrate his conversion, so in a spontaneous outcry to the others at the bar, he yelled:

Listen, everybody. Jesus Christ has saved me right here today. And I have promised Him to give my life to telling people about His love and power.

This calls for a celebration. Everybody come on. Bartender, set 'em up. The drinks are on me.

The Unorthodox New Beginning

Certainly that was unorthodox, but the man was sincere. And from that day, which terminated his life of drinking and carousing, he began his training for the ministry and has become a successful pastor and Christian leader.

What a miracle took place in that man when He suddenly became aware of *The Value Of*

People. He realized that God loved him, right there in that bar where he was.

When you discover that God values you as a woman, and that He has paid a supreme price for you because He loves you, you discover the principle that opens the gateway to true happiness, peace, success and fulfillment. That is what real *Life For Women* is, and it is for you — now.

Love Proved Your Value

It is wonderful when you get God's viewpoint, His attitude about a woman's life.

Here is some of what God says about you in the New Testament. I have personalized these verses for you.

So now you have been made right in God's sight because of what Jesus Christ your Lord has done for you.

He has brought you into this place of highest privilege where you now stand, and you confidently and joyfully look forward to actually becoming all that God has had in mind for you to be.

You are able to hold your head high, for you know how dearly God loves you.

Now you rejoice in your wonderful new relationship with God — all because of what your Lord Jesus Christ has done in dying for your sins making you a friend of God.[7]

Remember these three statements:

*He has brought you to this place of highest privilege.

*You joyfully look forward to becoming all that God has in mind for you to be.

*You rejoice in your wonderful new relationship — making you (-- a woman) a friend of God.

How God Valued A Villager

A dear village man who had a terrible rupture, and one lame leg, attended one of our crusades. The first night he came, he learned how God valued him so much that He gave His Son to redeem him. He believed the message and Jesus completely and instantly healed him.

The next night he carried his daughter to the crusade. She had been crippled from polio and could not walk. As she heard the Gospel, she too believed on the Lord and was saved. Then she was miraculously healed as her father had been. She could walk, run and jump as well as anyone.

Then the old man brought his insane sister. She had to be kept chained to a tree like a wild animal because she was totally deranged and physically dangerous.

Four men helped bring her to the crusade. They held her and kept her quiet during the meeting. As we taught, *the power of the Lord was present to heal.*[8] The evil spirits which had taken control of her mind went out of her and she was completely healed and restored by the power and the presence of Christ.

These remarkable miracles came to pass in this family through faith in God's word of promise. They discovered that God valued them and paid a price to redeem them to Him. He loved them and wanted to come and live with them.

The Principle Of
God's Value

The Value Of People is the message that gave that father faith in God. No one ever told him that he, a poor African villager, was valuable to God, that his paralyzed, helpless daughter was vital to God's plan, that his demented sister, foaming at the mouth and shrieking like a wild animal, was so valuable to God that He had paid for her to be restored to His *Life For Women.*

This is the principle that opened the door to a new and powerful faith in Christ and in His love. Discovering these truths enabled that dear man to call on the Lord with faith, and his entire family was blessed and restored to peace with God and to new vibrant physical health.

As a woman, when you discover the principle of your value to God and of His intense love for you, then you can become His co-worker and witness, helping others to discover this marvelous new life.

Behold My Hands! I Am Jesus!

In one of our crusades in India a young, arrogant, university student stood at the back of the crowd with folded arms, seething in anger. He wondered what he could do to drive these foreign teachers out of his town and to stop our influence on his people.

But as we preached about Jesus and then prayed, suddenly the Lord appeared to that young political activist. As Jesus looked straight into the young man's eyes, He opened His nail-pierced hands and said, *Behold my hands! I am Jesus!* Then with a soft smile and eyes of compassion, He disappeared.

The young man fell to his knees weeping and received Jesus Christ as his Lord and Master. He told the whole multitude what had happened to him and hundreds accepted the Lord.

That man realized the price God had paid to prove how He valued him. He discovered *The Value Of People.*

Having preached before multitudes in over 70 nations, I know something of the doctrines and teachings of the world's great religious founders — Mohammed, Buddha, Confucius and others.

Jesus Christ is the only one who died for His followers. He is the only one who loved them enough to lay down His life for them. He is the only one who rose from the dead and came back to carry on His ministry of love in and through those who believe on Him.

When He returned from the grave, He did not lecture them about His suffering.

He just showed them His hands and His side. He showed them the nailprints and the wound of the sword that was thrust through His body. He showed them the proof of *The Value Of People.*

That infinite value applies to every woman the same as it applies to every man.

Nailprints Proved His Love

His message was: *Peace be to you. Behold my hands and my feet, that it is I myself. He showed them His hands and his feet.*[9]

That is what He did to that young Hindu in our crusade in India. He opened His hands and said: *Behold my hands. I am Jesus.*

The nailprints were the proof of His love.

Jesus Christ is the only one who has nailprints in His hands. Jesus bears the eternal scars which prove how much God believes you and I are worth. As a woman, never allow any theologian or ecclesiastic to demean or depreciate your value to God or to obstruct or limit your ministry as His friend, His witness and His co-worker.

God values you. If you ever question it, remember His scars — the proof of the value He places on you today, just like you are. He loves you.

He proved it. You can trust His love. He paid the price to provide the ultimate of His divine *Life For Women* the same as He did for men.

Accepting Your Value

Now pray this prayer to the Lord.

DEAR LORD, I thank You for the good news which has come to me today through this book.

If You could come to a maniac like Kariuki in Kikuyuland, You can come to me right now.

When You shed Your blood and laid down Your life for my sins, You proved forever my VALUE as a human person. You cleared a path for me to come to God. You brought me back to You as Your friend so that I can experience Your LIFE forever.

There is nothing in my sinful life that is left standing against me, because I am fully convinced of the good news that Jesus died for me.

Thank You, Lord, for Your love.

I receive YOU, Lord Jesus, as my Savior and friend.

I rejoice in my wonderful new relationship with God through what Jesus did for me in dying for my sins.

I can lift my head high now, because I see the PROOF of how dearly You love me. I see the nailprints in Your hands which prove the value that You place on me.

Thank You for Your NEW LIFE that is now in me. Help me to share this good news with others so that they can be changed too.

In Jesus' name!

Amen!

NOW THAT YOU have been blessed with new life, make it count for God, and for others, by investing yourself to help reach others for Christ. The greatest reward in life is to know that you are a partner and a friend with God by sharing Christ with others.

Bible References:

1. Col.1:13-14 LB
2. Col.1:20-23 LB
3. 1Pe.1:25
4. Lu.5:17
5. Jn.2:23
6. Jn.6:2
7. Ro.5:1,2,5,11 LB
8. Lu.5:17
9. Lu.24:36,39-40

Wonderful miracles confirm Daisy's gospel message at the Surabaya Stadium. Top, Left: A crippled man is healed. Right: A woman discards her crutches. Below: A lady pushes her wheelchair (then asks Daisy to ride), to prove her miraculous healing by Christ's power.

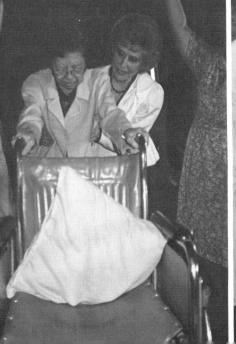

Dr. Daisy's National Women's Miracle Day
Rally at Stadium in Surabaya, Java.

Daisy Osborn addresses a multitude of women at her Java National Women's Miracle Day Rally in Surabaya. Thousands were lifted to new levels of self-esteem and of faith in Christ.

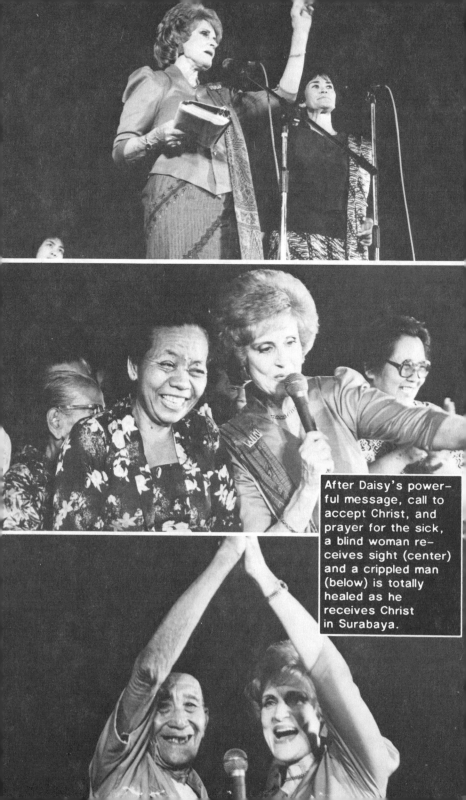

After Daisy's powerful message, call to accept Christ, and prayer for the sick, a blind woman receives sight (center) and a crippled man (below) is totally healed as he receives Christ in Surabaya.

IV

SUCCESS

FOR

WOMEN

MOTHER TERESA said, *With God and two pennies, I can do anything!*

After the Lord spoke to me in an audible voice, I decided to do something about the millions of hurting women in my world. I could not leave the evangelization of women to the men.

I cast myself, with all that I have and with all that I am, on Him, counting on Him to bless my life in helping millions of women to discover their individual dignity and destiny in His plan.

Christ is never limited in ministry through a woman, unless she chooses to limit Him herself.

Jesus wants to do through women the same things which He did through the body called Jesus of Nazareth. He has never changed. In you today, *Jesus is the same*[1] as He was in Bible days. That is the principle of *Success For Women.*

Chapter 4

SUCCESS FOR WOMEN

WHEN PEOPLE SEE a Christian woman, they see *CHRIST* in this century. They hear Christ speak, when she speaks. She is His representative, His ambassador. Jesus Christ in her wills to do the same things which He did inside the body called Jesus of Nazareth. Women are expressions of the Christ-life the same as men are. God wills *Success For Women* — spiritually, physically and materially.

I heard one of our State Governors speak recently. He pleaded for people to learn the secret of SUCCESS in life — to be interested in people; for human beings to cultivate common interests, to join in a common expression of good to all who are less privileged.

I said to myself: *What a tragedy if political leaders catch on to the secrets of success in life before Christian women do!*

I wondered how I could help more women discover for themselves loving ministries of productive achievement for the good of their world. This is the objective of real success for God's woman.

There is no life as satisfying as the one involved for the good of others.

Limits For Women?

For some reason, Christian tradition has limited women to a specifically disciplined framework of ministry which is politely, yet firmly restrained at a safe distance from what is appropriate for men. Church dogma interprets *ministry* very differently for women than it does for men.

Christian women in the church are expected to be saved, Spirit-filled and gifted by God. Yet their ministry is tightly circumscribed and arbitrarily limited to submissive and subservient roles.

Therefore their potential and their creative talents for ministry and leadership are rarely included in the community of believers.

Every Christian woman has a noble and a worthy reason to succeed in life. That reason is to be a partner and a co-worker with God in communicating the good news of Jesus Christ to hurting and needy people.

Preach to every creature is another way to say *communicate the good news to people.*

Develop the means and the methods of reaching out to your world in effective ministry. That requires money. Acquiring money calls for business expertise and creative enterprise in a competitive world that should be free of sexual prejudice and bigotry.

Can A Christ-Woman Express Christ?

When any woman becomes a Christian, she becomes a minister. She is a Christ-woman. Christ's nature becomes her nature. Her emotions become tuned to His. Christ's interests become her interests. Each Christian woman is another expression of Christ in human flesh. She experiences the real Christ-*Life For Women.*

When people see a Christian woman, they see Christ in this century. She is His representative, His ambassador.

Christ Jesus *came to seek and to save that which was lost.* [2] He came *not to be ministered to, but to minister.* [3] He taught us, as women, to do the same. *Whoever of you will be the chiefest shall be servant of all.* [4]

A Christian woman's mission and purpose in life is the same as Christ's. The compassion which drove the Christ of Galilee drives the same Christ who is inside you and me as women.

Christian *Success For Women* is living and doing the way Christ lived and did. We are to communicate the gospel to the unconverted, to our world of non-church goers.

Over 90 percent of society will never go to church. We, as women, must go out where the people are to witness and to win them there — as Jesus did; in the streets, market places, parks, roadsides, ball fields, tents, shops,

houses, auditoriums, assembly halls — wherever
there are people.[5]

Service To The Needy
Is Service To The King

Christian women pray for God to use them
in spiritual service. The only way to render
service to God is by helping and by ministering
to people. The most sacred and spiritual ministry any woman can have is her ministry to
people — to the poor, to the outcast, to the unconverted, to people in need — to God's creatures.

Service to the poorest of the poor is divine
service to the King of Kings! Ministering in the
filthiest gutters of human need is ministering in
the most sacred echelons of spiritual perfor-
mance.

We express our love to God by expressing
His love to people. We serve God by serving
people. We touch God by touching people. We
exalt and praise God by lifting people.

When a woman discovers this principle, and
when she embraces it for herself and practices
it in her life — without permitting herself to be
circumscribed by racial, economic, sexual, religious or cultural bias, she has learned the real
secret of *Success For Women*.

Christ's Love —
Mother Teresa's Faith

The eighth chapter of Mark is a powerful example of Christ's compassion expressed on behalf of people.

Mark says, *In those days, the multitude was very great.*[6] It is greater today. There are hundreds of millions of souls to be reached.

In verse 2, Christ says, *I have compassion on the multitude.* But what could be done to feed those thousands of hungry people?

When Mother Teresa told friends of her dream to establish a place where despairing and hopeless lepers could be loved and could find some dignity — at least in their death, she was ridiculed by those who knew that she had no money.

She asserted: *But I have two pennies!*

What can you do with two pennies? she was asked.

Gleaming with vital faith and moved with compassion, Mother Teresa asserted, *With God and two pennies, one can do anything!*

That must be what Jesus thought as He beheld the hungry multitude. He cared for them, and His compassion moved Him to do something about their needs.

If we, as women, care about hurting people,
the Jesus who is in us will, through the divine
energy of God at work within us, create a so-
lution for problems, healing of diseases, freedom from enslavement, hope for the despairing,
life for the dying.

As we choose to turn Christ loose inside us
— He can feed them through us.

Our commission is to *every creature.*

That seems to be an impossible task, except
that He has promised us: *Lo, I am with you always.* That is our power source. That is our
secret of *Success For Women.*

When God Touches What We Offer

Each of the four Gospels records the feeding of the 5,000 men — plus the women and the
children. Each one tells of the vital part which
a lad had in that miracle. He offered his five
loaves and two fishes to Christ to help meet the
need of the multitude, never dreaming that what
he had to offer would be touched by God and
would become sufficient to meet the enormous
needs of so many people.

How insignificant that lad's little lunch
looked when put up against the needs of thousands of hungry men, women and children!

It reminds me of what we offer to Christ
when it is weighed against the challenge of
reaching this generation with the gospel.

Five loaves and two fishes, given with purpose, were transformed by a miracle, a multitude of hungry people were fed. That is success!

When we do something to share, our act of love is transformed by a miracle that can give the Bread of Life to hungry souls.

No woman can feed thousands of people with only five loaves and two fishes without a miracle. Neither can any one of us reach *every creature* by our own efforts alone.

Jesus says, *give me what you have — I will bless it and multiply it by a miracle.* The result: *They did all eat and were filled.*[7]

What I AM And What I HAVE

When I contemplate the challenge of reaching the women of our world, I realize that this task is far too great for me to accomplish. But I cast myself, with all that I have and with all that I am, on Him, losing my all in His purpose, counting on Him to take what I am and what I have to offer, and to multiply it to bless the women and the men of my world, just as Christ took the five loaves and two fishes and fed that multitude.

As sure as Christ blessed that lad's gift to feed the multitude — plus giving him back 12 basketsful extra, in that same way Christ will touch what you offer and cause it to miraculously feed others with the Bread of Life — and you will discover an abundance of blessings left over for you.

If that child would have given those five
loaves to five hungry individuals, that would
have been a reasonable ministry, but no miracle
would have marked his gift. It would never
have been recorded in the Bible to inspire you
and me today.

Remember you never touch the resources of
God until you attempt the impossible.

Offer your talents to Christ, like the youth
offered to Him his five loaves and two fishes.
Plant of yourself to help feed *every creature* in
the *multitude* of this generation. Then expect a
miracle. That opens the doorway to *Success For
Women* the same as it does for men.

Be like a good woman farmer who plants
her seed in good soil. Expect a harvest of abundantly more than you sow. That is the secret of
success for any royal daughter in God's family.

Women Are Discovering

Are you willing to experience a material
miracle? Could it happen to you?

Let me tell you, it is happening to women
all across the world who are marking themselves as Partners in God's work. They are
grasping the biblical principles of *Success For
Women* today.

1. Women Partners are discovering that
God wills that they, as women, *PROSPER* (fi-
nancially as much as spiritually) *and that they
live in health, even as their souls prosper.*[8]

2. Women across the world are proving that if they *honor the Lord with their firstfruits,* He fulfills His word of promise and *fills their barns with PLENTY.*[9]

3. God's women are discovering that His word is a perpetual covenant for their own prosperity; that God who made all of the treasures of this earth wants women on His team to share them.

4. Women of God are becoming aware that God never created the wealth of this planet for the unconverted to monopolize; that it is *God who gives them power to get wealth;*[10] that *riches and wealth are the gift of God;*[11] that God has covenanted to make *you* (as a woman) *PLENTEOUS in goods,*[12] to *command His blessing upon your storehouses and in all that you set your hand to do.*[13]

5. Christian women are learning that when they offer their seed-gifts or their firstfruits for sharing Christ with their world, God has contracted in His word to *bless the fruit of their ground and cattle, to increase their basket and their store,*[14] and to actually *make them PLENTEOUS in every work.*[15]

6. Women are proving that God's will for them is unchanged today about money, that *as long as they seek the Lord, God makes them to PROSPER;*[16] that God *will give them riches, wealth and honor.*[17]

7. Women are becoming aware that every time they plant their firstfruits or their seed-

gifts in the good soil of God's will which is
sharing Christ with others, *it SHALL be given
back to them; good measure, pressed down,
shaken together and running over.*[18]

New Dimensions Of Self-Value

Because of God's established law of sowing
and reaping, every woman farmer expects to
reap much more than she sowed.

Because of God's unchangeable promises,
your seed-gift or your firstfruits planted as
seed-money in the fertile soil of God's work,
will miraculously produce a harvest of souls,
PLUS they will produce an abundant increase to
prosper YOU with His material blessings in
YOUR life at home.

Women of faith and of vision can exercise
their right of choice and release themselves
from the traditional limits imposed by a male-
dominated clergy system, and reach far beyond
the confines of restricted sanctuaries. Women
can break through the sectarian walls which
have restrained them in ministry, involving
themselves out in the arena of real human life,
discovering for themselves new dimensions of
Christian achievement and of self-value in dynamic and productive *Success For Women.*

Jesus said, *launch out into the deep* — not
into the depths of spiritual ecstasy, but out into
the depths of human misery; out where the despairing people are. That is where God's creative women discover true success, happiness and
meaningful achievement.

Christ Unlimited In Women

I have mentioned the 25th chapter of Matthew earlier in this book. I refer to it again because of its clear focus of the standard by which every woman's life will be weighed. It will be according to whether or not she fed the hungry, gave drink to the thirsty, clothed the naked, visited the sick and the prisoners.

Christ's immortal words are: *Inasmuch as you have done it to one of the least of these, my kinspeople, you have done it to me.*[19]

Jesus said, the hungry, the thirsty, the naked, the sick, the captive people are His brothers, His sisters. What we do to people, we do to Christ.

When we love and serve people, we love and serve Christ.

When we visit the prisoners, the shut-ins and the sick, we visit Christ.

We cannot see God or touch or handle Him. We can only express our devotion and our love to Him (whom we cannot see) by expressing His love and compassion to people (whom we can see).

When we receive Christ, He lives in us and once more becomes *God in the flesh* — through us, as women the same as He does through men. We are His body now. He walks in us. He speaks and ministers through us. He is not

limited by our social status, by our race or by
our sex, unless we allow Him to be.

Our body is His temple. Christ is our Life!
He does, through us as women, the same things
that He did through the body they called Jesus
of Nazareth.

The Lord's presence in a human person is
not qualified sexually. His ministry through a
woman is no different than it is through a man,
unless she chooses to restrict His expression
through her. For some reason, religious dogmas
have almost obscured this truth from Bible-be-
lieving women.

Today, women are on the rise in business,
in economics, in education, in politics, in science, in medicine and in almost every field of
human endeavor and achievement.

If there was ever an opportunity for God's
women to arise into action, it is now! Grasp
the biblical principles of *Success For Women.*
Resolve to share and to express the Christ-life
to *every creature* in whatever way God im-
presses or inspires you — as a *goer* as well as
a *sender.*

This is what Jesus was talking about when
He said: *Go to all the world and preach the
gospel to every creature — and lo I am with you
always!* That is His commission to every woman believer the same as it is to every man
believer. Women have the same biblical right to
act on Christ's words that men have.

Jesus wants to do through women the same things which He did through the body called Jesus of Nazareth. He has never changed. In you today, *Jesus is the same*[20] as He was in Bible days. That is the principle of *Success For Women*.

Women As God's Partners

As a woman believer, let Christ minister through you to fulfill all of His will. Purpose to allow Him freedom in your life to be all that He wills to be through you.

Remember, His will to reach *every creature* is impossible — without a miracle. So in order to develop your life with Christ and to share as His team-mate in material blessings the same as in spiritual or physical blessings, allow Him to guide you into enterprising endeavors. Then learn to sow your firstfruits or your seed-money in His work, and watch Him produce the miracle and multiply your seed-gifts like He multiplies wheat seed, or like He multiplied the lad's lunch.

To be part of God's miracle, you may have to plant what you need. The lad did. He needed that lunch for himself. But he placed it in Christ's hand. Then the miracle took place. It is very vital that you embrace, for yourself — a woman, the biblical promises set forth in this book. They will enrich and build your faith, motivating you to take your rightful place as a daughter in God's family — one who has learned, the principles of God's *Success For Women*.

Faith In Action

God promises that *your barns SHALL be filled with PLENTY*, because *God SHALL supply ALL YOUR NEED.*[21]   When *you* give, *it SHALL BE given to you.*[22] *These scriptures cannot be broken.*[23]   *Has God said; shall He not do it? Has He spoken; shall He not make it good?*[24]

God cannot break His covenant for *your* prosperity and for your success.[25]

By setting firstfruits of your increase and by investing it in His work of sharing Christ with people, you prove God by acting on His word. The only time in all of the Bible that He asks you to prove Him, concerns your money.[26] That shows how God regards the money over which He makes you the steward. When you seed part of your money in God's work, you are seeding part of your life in His plan.

He promises to open heaven's windows and to return so much more than you gave that you will not be prepared to receive it.[27]

God will do a material miracle to make good His word in your life. But best of all, you will be identified in His work of sharing Christ with others.

This is what I call the ultimate in real *Success For Women*.

Bible References:

1. He.13:8
2. Lu.19:10

3. Mk.10:45
4. Mk.10:44
5. Be sure to get our books, Soulwinning and Outside the Sanctuary, which have seeded the worldwide revival of evangelism out where the people are.
6. Mk.8:1
7. Mk.6:42
8. 3Jn.1:2
9. Pr.3:9-10
10. De.8:18
11. Ec.5:19
12. De.28:11
13. De.28:8
14. De.28:4-5
15. De.30:9
16. 2Ch.26:5
17. 2Ch.1:12
18. Lu.6:38
19. Mt.25:40
20. He.13:8
21. Ph.4:19
22. Lu.6:38
23. Jn.10:35
24. Nu.23:19
25. Ps.89:34
26. Mal.3:10
27. Mal.3:10

Daisy gives keynote address at her National Conference in Adelaide, Australia.

Daisy and T.L.'s daughter, LaDonna, preaches at International Gospel Center at Tulsa, OK, where she is the pastor.

V

A

WOMAN'S

DESIRES

GOD WANTS YOU, as His royal daughter to realize that within you is the possibility to shed the cloak of failure, to escape the negative syndrome of discouragement to break with the demoralizing dogmas of defeat, to get out of the boredom of conformity and to go for life in abundance — whether the majority of women do it or not.

No woman believer should be subordinated in life without personal means, without material achievements, without the self-pride of personal enterprise and without the self-esteem and the dignity of realizing personal success. *Ascend To Your Desires* and dare to tackle life. Harness the abilities of God within you. Embrace the fact that as He is, so are you (a woman) in this world.[1]

If your desires are supposed to be suppressed and are never allowed to motivate you to productive and creative action, you will die in nothingness and emptiness, without purpose or significance or fulfillment.

As God's women, we are *heirs of God, joint-heirs with Jesus Christ*[2] as much as men are.

When you recognize God at work in you as a woman, you begin to rise, to climb, to grow. You dare to tackle life, to harness the abilities of God within you and to go for achievement and success just like any believing man does.

Chapter 5

A WOMAN'S DESIRES

A WOMAN'S YEARNING POWER is more important than her earning power.

Women who succeed in life focus on the direction they desire to go and refuse the restrictive limit-mentality which society tends to impose upon them.

Recognize that *God is at work within you, helping you to want what He wants*[3] to desire what He desires.

I have published these vital ideas to encourage you, as a woman, and to motivate you to never again allow people, or systems, or traditions or culture to discredit your dreams, to dampen your ambitions or to suppress your aspirations.

As a woman, created in God's image, redeemed, restored and re-birthed as His partner, here are three basic steps for the restructuring of *Life For Women.*

Three Resolves For Women

Commit yourself to these three progressive resolves which will lift you out of female mediocrity and set you on your new road to achievement, fulfillment and distinction in life:

1st: Dream beyond what seems possible to you.

2nd: Desire what you dream about.

3rd: Drive for your dreams.

Desire to be more than the average woman settles for. A common characteristic of all winners is that they desire to achieve.

In Christian tradition, ones desire-power is usually interpreted as carnal ambition, as destructive pride or as fleshly lust of some kind. Believers and especially women are badgered about *the lust of the flesh, the lust of the eyes and the pride of life.*[4] This negative emphasis on your desires inhibits your vital drive to succeed in life.

When God is at work in you through Christ, the force of intense desire in you has a miraculous way of releasing creative energy, and an almost supernatural pull toward what you yearn for.

What do you, as a woman, want out of life with all of your heart? *A Woman's Desires,* when she has embraced the Christ-life, are as legitimate and as worthy as a believing man's are.

Is it wrong for a woman to desire to do things, to be somebody, to have something?

Helen Keller said, *We can do anything if we desire enough to do it, and if we stick to it!*

For women, religion has emphasized surrender and humility; it has sanctified resignation, submission and abandonment; but it has neglected the virtues of positivism, of faith, of productivity, of success and of accomplishment and these compose the substance and the expression of God's intended *Life For Women.*

Common sense tells us that God never intended for the wealth which He created in this world to be monopolized only by men. He never intended for men to be the controllers of all material blessings. He gave to Eve as well as to Adam His blessing, and told them both to *subdue the earth* and to *have dominion* over it.[5]

No woman believer should be subordinated in life without private means, without material achievements, without the self-pride of personal enterprise and without the self-esteem and the dignity of realizing individual success. A woman desires expression and fulfillment as much as does a man.

As a woman, learn to release your faith; allow yourself to sincerely desire the good things which God has created in your world. Believe that they are placed here for you — in partnership with Him, to enjoy and to use for the betterment of your world. Know that your desire is God's desire being expressed in and through you.

God says to women the same as to men: *Listen to Me and you will have a long, good life. Carry out My instructions, for they will lead you to real living.*[6]   That is what I call *Life For Women.*

Your Source Is UNlimited

A primitive village woman who beats the dirt from the family's clothes on a rock with a wood stick at the river side, does not know to desire a high-tech washing machine. But once she hears about it, new ideas fill her mind. Her ambition is fired. She desires a better life. *A Woman's Desires* are as authentic and as warranted as a man's are.

The purpose of this book is to inspire your desire for a better life in Christ — to His abundant *Life For Women.*

Every good gift and every perfect gift is from above and comes from the Father[7] — your Father, because you are His royal daughter.

From the day God created Adam and Eve in a garden of abundance, happiness, health and fulfillment, He has never changed His mind about women.

You were born to live in God's dream, with His lifestyle. You have the same miraculous capacity to think and to plan, to ponder and to imagine, to believe and to progress as any man has. God wants you as a member of His royal household to use those capacities.

When you recognize God at work in you as a woman, you begin to rise, to climb, to grow. You dare to tackle life, to harness the abilities of God within you and to go for achievement and success — just like any believing man does.

The Bible teaches that God rewards faith. *Anyone who comes to God must believe that He is, and that He is a rewarder of them that diligently seek Him.*[8]

Your Faith Is Your Desire
Turned Godward

God wants you, as His noble daughter, to realize that within you is the possibility to shed the cloak of failure, to escape the negative syndrome of discouragement, to break with the demoralizing dogmas of defeat, and to go for life in abundance.

God wants you to have His best in life, but He must wait until you desire it, before He can give it to you.

His entire design is; 1) to make His life and abundant blessings available — as His free gifts of love, 2) to send forth His word of promise concerning those blessings so that everyone may know about them, and 3) to respond and to fulfill, or to materialize those blessings for everyone who believes His promises and who sincerely reaches out to Him for them.

That is why Jesus came with God's message of Good News and told us to *ask* and to *seek* and to *knock*, promising response to *everyone who asks,* and who *seeks,* or who *knocks,*[9] meaning everyone who desires these blessings from God.

A Woman's Desires in reaching out for a better and a fuller material life for God's glory, are as fundamental and as right as any man's are. They should be asserted and pursued with the same legitimacy and sanction as a man's. Desire-power is creative power.

When a blind man cried out to Jesus, He stopped and asked him, *What do you want* (or desire) *Me to do for you?*[10] He desired his sight and he received it.

Jesus said to a woman who intensely desired Him to heal her daughter — and who would not give up: *Be it unto you even as you will.*[11] In contemporary language, He was saying, it is done, as you desire. And the girl was healed.

The Bible says: *Delight yourself in the Lord; and He will give you the desires of your heart. You will inherit the earth. God will exalt you to inherit the land*[12] — here, now. Those promises apply to you as a woman the same as they apply to any man.

Good News For Women

The true message of the Bible is good news for women and men alike.

I. Peace with God is GOOD.

No woman was ever created for guilt and fear. God's plan for you offers inner peace and tranquility[13] — now.

He wants you to have that happiness, but He waits until your desire is turned to His desire.

II. Physical health is GOOD.

No daughter in God's family was ever made to suffer pain, disease or disability. God's plan for you includes healing and soundness[14] — now.

He yearns for you to walk in His boundless health. But He must wait until you desire His health in you.

III. Material prosperity is GOOD.

No woman of God was ever created for poverty and deprivation. God's plan for you *includes prosperity, success and abundant living*[15] — now.

He wills all of His material abundance and blessings for you. But He must wait until you release yourself from the restricting limits which culture and religions have set for women.

When the fire of desire burns in you for material achievement in this world, so that you can be more effective as God's partner in helping people, then things begin to happen for you.

Jesus said, *Whatever you desire, when you pray, believe that you receive them, and you will have them.*[16]

God has given to you and to me the equivalent of a blank check. We are free to fill it in, and to draw on His unlimited resources.

That is what we do when we accept His opinion
of us and begin to really believe in His *Life
For Women.*

The Negative Accentuated

When my husband, T.L. Osborn, and I re-
searched what theologians had to say about desire, we found volumes written about its evil;
how it is condemned, judged, censured and pe-
nalized.

We knew that to desire riches or wealth or
any other thing out of greed, jealousy, avarice
or lust was wrong and destructive.

We knew about Ahab's greed for Naboth's
vineyard, about Joseph's brothers selling him because of envy and jealousy, about David's lust
for Bathsheba, about the rich man who heaped
his wealth to consume it in riotous living, about
Judas and his self-destruction over greed for a
petty thirty pieces of silver.

We knew hundreds of reasons to warn
women about the evil of wrong desire. But we
could find very little in theology that encourages
women to desire the good things God has created on this planet for them. Practically nothing
in theology transmits God's original message and
blessing to women; to exercise their prerogative,
along with men, and to *subdue* the earth and to
have dominion over it.[17]

It is nonsense to acquiesce to the position
that God's wealth on this earth is placed here
solely for men to monopolize. He gave that

blessing and command to the woman the same as to the man. It takes *both* to *be fruitful, and multiply, and replenish the earth.*[18] *Both* are to *subdue* the earth and to *have dominion over it and over every living thing that moves on earth.*

Dare To Desire

In a four-point, mini-resumé of God's redemptive plan, here is the essence of what God wants for you.

1. He wants what He wanted in the beginning. He wanted Adam and Eve to be happy, healthy, productive, and to live in abundance.

2. Then Satan tempted them. They rejected God's integrity, and forfeited the lifestyle and the riches which God created for them.

3. But God loved human persons too much to see them languish in poverty, loneliness, guilt and deterioration.

4. God gave Jesus, His Son, to come and to assume the penalty of every person's sins. He made only one condition for you as a woman: If you would believe on Him, you would be justified as though you had never sinned. Then God could live in you again, and all that had been forfeited would be restored to you, and you would be restored to God again as His partner and friend.

Identify with what Christ did for you as a woman, and believe that you receive God's *Life For Women* again.

Life Is God's Idea

Jesus died to redeem and to restore you as a woman, to God. He justified you from all of your past, and brought you back to God as though nothing ever stood between you and Him.

He wants to give back to you every blessing, every provision and every gift of abundance which He created for humanity in the beginning.

Now God offers everything to fulfill your happiness, prosperity, health and abundant living. *All (things) are yours, and you are Christ's; and Christ is God's.*[19] That is for you as a woman.

If you believe in God's redemptive plan, you can have whatever you desire.

All things are possible to anyone who believes.[20]

Whatever you desire when you pray, believe that you receive them and you will have them.[21]

The desire of the righteous will be granted.[22]

Delight yourself in the Lord and He will give you the desires of your heart.[23]

Each one of these promises — and so many others, are for you as a woman as much as they are for any man.

Because of sermonizers who stress the negative side of desire, women (and many men) usually practice suppressing their ambitions.

One of the cardinal doctrines of Hinduism is to suppress all desire for any blessing, or status, or happiness, or success in life.

Buddha taught that human persons could achieve a level of mental control where all desires in life would be neutralized. He called this *Nirvana* or desirelessness.

But the very yearning for the state of desirelessness is in itself desire. In fact, Hindus may spend a lifetime struggling for this paradise of neutrality. It is like trying to cure a headache by severing one's head.

We Are Created With Desire

If your desires are supposed to be suppressed and are never allowed to motivate you to productive and creative action, you will die in nothingness and emptiness, without purpose or significance or fulfillment.

As God's women, we are *heirs of God, joint-heirs with Jesus Christ* [24] as much as men are.

We, as women, are heirs of the Kingdom of God which He has promised to them that love Him.[25]

God, through Christ *has made us* (as women) *kings* (or queens) *and priests unto God.*[26] We are rulers. We have authority. We have dignity. We have a commission. We are believers, ambassadors, representatives, co-laborers with God, with the power to act in Christ's name as men believers have.

It is time for God's royal daughters to believe and to confess that we are what God is in us — to embrace the fact that, *as He IS, so ARE WE in this world.*[27]

To believe for something or to pray for something is to desire it. Prayer is desire turned heavenward. *The desire of the righteous is only good.*[28] When God is alive in you, your desires are His desires.

Doctrine Of Poverty

Religion, in its countless species, invariably links poverty with godliness, suffering with piety, burdens with humility and lack with holiness — especially for women.

Emerson, the great American philosopher, says that from the time he was a lad, he wanted to write an essay exposing theology that indoctrinates people against desiring material success, achievement, and prosperity.

He was shocked at the pundits and preachers who always emphasize that the wicked should be successful in this world; but that Christians should prove their humility by living lives of misery.

In other words, Emerson said, preachers applaud riches for the righteous — *in heaven,* but deplore material prosperity for them here *on earth.*

He said, in essence, they are teaching Christians to say:

It is a sin to be rich here on earth. I shall not sin now, but I shall sin in heaven; I would like to sin now, but I shall get my revenge later.

Saved For Significance

It has never been right to tell women to acquiesce in subjugated nothingness while men dominate the control of all economic and material property or status.

The wealth which God created is to achieve and to be put to work for the good of people through the instrumentality of women as well as of men.

Should believing women refuse to educate and discipline themselves, and never apply their talents to achieve material success when it can mean so much in helping people?

Angels announced Christ's coming by saying, *We have glad tidings of great joy for ALL people. Behold a savior is born!*[29]

A Savior for whom, and from what?

The *glad tidings* is that Christ came as the Savior from the judgment of sins, from the curse of deterioration, self-deprecation and insignificance, from sickness and disease, from poverty and failure, from mediocrity and humiliation, from disobedience and death.

Jesus came as a woman's *Savior* from the negativism of religion that demoralizes and negates her human personhood.

Jesus healed a poor woman *who had a spirit of infirmity eighteen years, and could in no wise lift up herself.*[30] The religious crowd yelled: It's the wrong day! Leave her handicapped and crippled! Respect the sabbath![31]

They cared more for their laws than they did for a poor woman's impaired body.

Jesus raised a man from the dead who had been in his tomb for four days. The religious crowd never glorified God but recoiled and took counsel to kill Jesus, lest the people should believe on Him.[32]

They preferred to ignore the miracle and to kill the Master rather than to risk losing their monopoly over the people.

Jesus came across a naked maniac — a wild man. The religious crowd had no interest in him, but left him to his torment.

Jesus restored his mind and gave him a position of honor. He sent him to the ten towns known as the Decapolis to represent Him personally.[33]

Jesus met an unclean leper. The religious crowd left him to his fate. But Jesus cleansed him so that he could have honor and respect as a proper citizen again.[34]

They brought a woman to Jesus who had been taken in the act of adultery. The religious crowd wanted to stone her to death for breaking the law.

Jesus treated her like a lady and restored her self-esteem by forgiving her sins.[35]

Jesus Christ is a lifter of women, a healer, a restorer of human persons. He wants to restore your faith in life, if circumstances have broken your will.

You Count With God

If you have been blind to your value or to the possibilities around you, Jesus Christ will open your eyes to see a dozen solutions to problems you thought were insurmountable.

Your ears may have been stopped. Perhaps you missed the answers in life. The Lord will miraculously open your ears and you will hear what counts for life's best.

You may have been demoralized until you withdrew in surrender, in submission and in humiliation. Jesus will stand up inside of you and cause you to walk with dignity in life, and succeed where you failed before.

As a woman, embrace these verses personally:

YOU are the SALT of the earth. [36]

YOU are the LIGHT of the world. [37]

Follow Me and I will MAKE you. [38]

YOUR sins are forgiven. [39]

RISE UP and walk. [40] Never hang your head in shame again.

Stretch forth YOUR hand. [41]

R-E-A-C-H OUT — beyond your self as a woman.

Only BELIEVE. [42]

HAVE FAITH all things are possible. [43]

God gives hope to the hopeless and power to the powerless; He is good to all who come to Him and call upon Him. Desire the good which He has created for you.

Help Yourself To God's Lifestyle

For God to live in you, as a woman, He wants good things to abound in your life. It is right for you, as one of God's royal daughters, to desire the material blessings He has put within your reach. *A Woman's Desires* are as valid and as pertinent to *Life For Women* as a man's are to life for man.

All that God created for His children, in the beginning, is now restored to you through Jesus Christ. Desire what He offers.

Help Yourself

Jesus saw a crippled man who had been unable to walk for 38 years. Jesus asked him: *Do you desire to be made whole?*[44] He asks that of you, now.

Are you dissatisfied with life as it is? Do you want a better way? Do you desire a fuller life? Are you willing to be prosperous and successful and to assume the responsibility of administering wealth and success for your own good and for the good of people?

The crippled man blamed others for his 38 year plight. He said that no one would help him to get well.[45]

Jesus said, in essence: Help yourself! Get up! Carry your bed! Walk![46]

The man got up and walked and was whole again.

Decide what you desire and resolve to appropriate it! You can have or do or be anything that you desire.

Through you, God wants to make a better world in you and around you. Your action is motivated only by what you want. When there is no desire, no choice is made, no decision is taken, no action is performed. Without the *want to* there is no *will to*.

Oath Of Prosperity

If your desire is suppressed by negative religious teaching, then you will waste your life and die in resignation and in pious submission.

You will be like so many women who have bound themselves with an oath of poverty. God never planned for anyone to do that. Decide today to take an oath of prosperity and say:

> *As a woman, I vow never to be poor and indigent, since my Father created the wealth of this planet for me to enjoy and to use in His service.*

> *As a woman, I vow never to be unable to reach out and to lift others who are in need. God is in me and He is rich.*

> *As a woman, I vow to always appropriate God's blessings in life so that I can enjoy His abundance myself, and so that I can share His abundance with others in need.*

> *As a woman, I vow to remember that the Lord is my Shepherd; I will not want. My cup runs over.*[47]

Nothing Is Too Good For You

Take these promises into your heart and embrace them now. I have personalized them for you as a woman.

No good thing will He withhold from any woman who walks uprightly before Him.[48]

I wish ABOVE ALL THINGS that you may prosper and be in health even as her soul prospers.[49]

Jesus said, I have come so that women may have life, and that they may live in abundance.[50]

Instead of shame and dishonor, women will have a double portion of prosperity and everlasting joy. All will realize that you are a woman God has blessed.[51]

See yourself as a royal daughter in God's family with His riches, His power and His love at work in you and through you.

Woman's Resolve

Let a deep resolve form inside of you that says:

As a woman, I am through with failure, mediocrity, sickness and poverty.

As a woman, I am through with jealousy, resentment, fear and guilt.

As a woman, I am tired of loneliness and disappointment; of bills and mortgages.

As a woman, the fire of desire is burning in me for a better life, better health, more love, greater success, a closer relationship with God, prosperity, peace and happiness.

Recognize that those desires are God working in you to will and to do His good pleasure.[52]

Jesus At Work In You

Jesus said: *The works that I do, you will do also.*[53]   Let the real Jesus stand up in you and come alive!   Whatever He is, He is all of that in you!

He touched lepers and they became clean.[54]

He touched blind eyes and sight was restored.[55]

He touched crippled and lame people and they walked.[56]

He touched weary and demoralized people and they received new life.[57]

He touched people with fever and they became normal again.[58]

He touched people with fear and they were confident again.[59]

He touched deaf-mutes and they could hear and speak.[60]

He touched wounded people and they were instantly healed.[61]

That is what He yearns to do in you as a woman, so expand your faith and allow Him to be all that He is through you. Reach out and *become all that God has had in mind for you to be.*[62]

As you read this book, you will never be the same woman again. It is planting good seeds in the fertile soil of your life. Be sure to get all of the books I have written, because each of them will strengthen your faith as a woman, even more.

Become active in some form of people-helping ministry in your world. You are a *bonafide,* authorized partner with God in His work of blessing people. He promises to return to you a harvest of much more than you ever plant,[63] and to bless everything you put your hand to do.

May His presence at work in you give you the faith and the courage *to be all that God has in mind for you to be.*[64]

Bible References: Page 130

Dr. Daisy preaches and ministers at Women's Conference — Nigeria.

Daisy teaches and ministers at Osborn Soulwinners' Institute — Kenya.

Daisy preaches and ministers at Mission Convention — Norway.

Daisy preaches and ministers at National Women's Conference — USA.

Bible References:

1. 1Jn.4:17
   Ph.2:13
2. Ro.8:17
3. Ph.2:13
4. 1Jn.2:16
5. Ge.1:28
6. Pr.4:10,13 LB
7. Ja.1:17
8. He.11:6
9. Mk.7:8
10. Mk.10:51 LB
11. Mt.15:28
12. Ps.37:4,9,34
13. 2Co.5:21
   1Pe.2:24
14. 3Jn.1:2
   Ex.15:26
   Mt.8:17
   Is.53:5
15. Ps.34:10
   Mk.10:29-30
   Jn.10:10
   Ac.8:18
   Ac.28:11
   Ph.4:19

16. Mk.11:24
17. Ge.1:28
18. Ge.1:28
19. 1Co.3:22-23
20. Mk.9:23
21. Mk.11:24
22. Pr.10:24
23. Ps.37:4
24. Ro.8:17
25. Ja.2:5
26. Re.1:6;5:10
27. 1Jn.4:17
28. Pr.11:23
29. Lu.2:10-11
30. Lu.13:11
31. Lu.13:14
32. Jn.11:48,53
33. Mk.5:1-20
34. Mk.1:40-45
35. Jn.8:4-11
36. Mt.5:13
37. Mt.5:14
38. Mt.4:19
39. Mk.2:5
   Ps.103:3

40. Lu.5:23
41. Mk.3:5
42. Lu.8:50
43. Mk.9:23
44. Jn.5:6
45. Jn.5:7
46. Jn.5:8
47. Ps.23:1,5
48. Ps.84:11
49. 3Jn.2
50. Jn.10:10
51. Je.33:6,8-9
52. Ph.2:13
53. Jn.14:12
54. Mk.1:40
55. Mt.9:29
56. Mk.6:55-56
57. Mt.14:36
58. Mt.8:15
59. Mt.17:7
60. Mk.7:33
61. Lu.22:51
62. Ro.5:2 LB
63. Lu.6:38
64. Ro.5:2

VI

SEEDS

OF

GOLD

THESE *Seeds Of Gold* will be a foundation for new faith and power in your life, as you resolve *to become all that God had in mind for you* (as a woman) *to be.*[1]

Women today cannot afford to bow before the chauvinistic dictums of a male clergy. Christ in a woman is not qualified socially, racially or sexually.

Four ways for women to practice the presence of Jesus in their lives. Also, the simple secret to receiving the blessings of health, happiness, love and success.

A gold mine of riches for YOURSELF and for your loved ones.

Jesus is present in your life every moment. Since you are His body, He wants to express Himself and to carry out His mission of love to others through you, as a woman. Practice letting Him do it.

He has no hands but our hands
To do His work today.

He has no feet but our feet
To lead us on His way.

He has no tongue but our tongue
To tell the world He died.

He has no help but our help
To bring them to His side.

Chapter 6

SEEDS OF GOLD

WHY DOES EACH woman have special abilities to do certain things best? Why do women often abandon hope of getting good things from God or of achieving personal success in life?

These *Seeds Of Gold* will be a foundation for new faith and power in your life, as you resolve to become all that God had in mind for you (as a woman) to be.[2]

There are basic needs in each woman's life, and there is a simple secret to receiving the blessings which God planned for women — blessings such as health, happiness, love, success, etc.

When you, as a woman, discover your roots in God, you will find a gold mine of divine riches for yourself and for your loved ones.

In the third century, Cyprian, the Bishop of Carthage, wrote to his Roman friend Donatus: *It is a bad world, Donatus, an incredibly bad world. But I have discovered in the midst of it a quiet and holy people who have learned a great secret. They have found a joy which is a thousand times better than any of the pleasures of our sinful life. They are despised and persecuted, but they do not care. They have overcome the world. These people, Donatus, are Christians and I am one of them.*

If you have embraced Christ as your Savior, then you too, are one of those overcomers in life — one of those wonderful Christians.

Principles Of Christian Living

Sermonizers and theological pontificates have often been the enemies of women rather than their examples. With their masculinized vocabulary, they have usually ignored women, or if their existence is ever acknowledged, it is usually within a context of reinforcing traditional restraints or limits upon their lifestyles.

But a yet greater injustice for women has been to treat God's word as though it were addressed principally to men. It is not! Every word and each biblical promise is as though God were speaking to women personally, the same as to men.

Women are no longer barred from education or from participation in the worlds of business, of science, of economics, of industry, of politics, of government, or of trade. Only in religion are they restrained by this medieval discrimination.

But since women are no longer illiterate, they can now read the Bible for themselves, and accept it personally; women can believe it and to act upon God's word spoken to them in exactly the same way that any man would be expected to do.

Women today can no longer afford to bow to the chauvinistic dictums of a male clergy. Women today can read God's word. As faith is birthed in their hearts through His word, women can act, and they can experience Jesus Christ at work in and through them. Christ in a woman is never qualified socially, racially or sexually.

I have published these *Seeds Of Gold* for you, as a woman. They will encourage you to follow Christ *who gave you a share in His very own life, for He forgave all your sins, and blotted out the charges proved against you ... God took the list of* (your) *sins and destroyed it by nailing it to Christ's cross. In this way He took away Satan's power to accuse you.*[3]

Now, *you are living a brand new kind of life that is continually learning more and more of what is right, and trying constantly to be more and more like Christ who created this new life within you.*[4]

In this new life, your nationality or race or education or social position (and we could add, *or sex) is unimportant; such things mean nothing. Whether you have Christ is what matters, and He is equally available to all.*[5]   Because *we are no longer Jews or Greeks or slaves or free or even men or women, but we are all the same — we are Christians; we are one in Christ Jesus.*[6]

We who believe (that included you as a woman, if you are a believer) *are carefully joined together with Christ ... and with each other by the Spirit, and are part of this dwelling place of God.*[7]

So as a woman, *don't let others spoil your faith and joy with their philosophies ... built on men's thoughts and ideas, instead of on what Christ has said. For in Christ* (for a woman as well as for a man) *there is all of God in a human body. So you have everything when you have Christ, and you* (as a woman) *are filled with God through your union with Christ. He is the highest Ruler, with authority over every other power.*[8] *All God gives to His Son Jesus is now yours too.*[9]

Never forget, that as a woman, *because of your faith, God has brought you into this place of highest privilege where you now stand, and you confidently and joyfully look forward to actually becoming all that God has in mind for you to be.*[10].

As an intelligent woman of God, saved through Christ and called to be His empowered *witness,*[11] His *ambassador,*[12] His *co-laborer,*[13] and His *joint-heir,*[14] embrace these *Seeds Of Gold* and claim them for yourself, as a *follower of God.*[15]

A vital step in your following the Lord is your fellowship with other Christians.

The Bible teaches that *You are the body of Christ, and members in particular;*[16] that all believers are to *become more and more in every way like Christ who is the head of His body, the church. Under His direction the whole body is fitted together perfectly, and each part in its own special way helps the other parts, so that the whole body is healthy and growing and full of love.*[17]

Paul says of individual Christians — of women believers as well as of men believers: *Some of us have been given special ability as apostles; to others Christ has given the gift of being able to preach well; some have special ability in winning people to Christ, helping them to trust Him as their Savior; still others have a gift for caring for God's people as a shepherd does his sheep, leading and teaching them in the ways of God.*

Why is it He gives us these special abilities to do certain things best? It is that God's people will be equipped to do better work for Him, building up the church, the body of Christ, to a position of strength and maturity; until finally we all believe alike about our salvation and about our Savior, God's Son, and all become full-grown in the Lord — yes, to the point of being filled full with Christ.[18]

We will lovingly follow the truth at all times — speaking truly, living truly — and so become more and more like Christ who is the head of His body, the church.[19]

And now you have become living building-stones for God's use in building His house. What's more, you are His holy priests; so come to Him — (you who are acceptable to Him because of Jesus Christ) — and offer to God those things that please Him.[20]

And so, I plead with you to give your bodies to God. Let them be a living sacrifice, holy — the kind He can accept. When you think of what He has done for you, is this too much to ask?

Don't copy the behavior and customs of this world, but be a new and different person with a fresh newness in all you do and think.

Then you will learn from your own experience how His ways will really satisfy you.[21]

Be honest in your estimate of yourselves, measuring your value by how much faith God has given you.

Just as there are many parts to our bodies, so it is with Christ's body. We are all parts of it, and it takes every one of us to make it complete, for we each have different work to do.

So we belong to each other, and each needs all the others.

God has given each of us the ability to do certain things well.

So if God has given you the ability to prophesy, then prophesy whenever you can — as often as your faith is strong enough to receive a message from God.

If your gift is that of serving others, serve them well.

If you are a teacher, do a good job of teaching.

If you are a preacher, see to it that your sermons are strong and helpful.

If God has given you money, be generous in helping others with it.

If God has given you administrative ability and put you in charge of the work of others, take the responsibility seriously.

Those who offer comfort to the sorrowing should do so with Christian cheer.

Don't just pretend that you love others: really love them.

Hate what is wrong.

Stand on the side of the good.

Love each other with brotherly and sisterly affection and take delight in honoring each other.

Never be lazy in your work, but serve the Lord enthusiastically.

Be glad for all God is planning for you.

Be patient in trouble, and prayerful always.

When God's children are in need, you be the one to help them out.

And get in the habit of inviting guests home for dinner or, if they need lodging, for the night.

If people mistreat you because you are a Christian, don't curse them; pray that God will bless them.

When others are happy, be happy with them. If they are sad, share their sorrow.

Work happily together. Don't try to act big. Don't try to get into the good graces of important people, but enjoy the company of ordinary folks. And don't think you know it all.

Never pay back evil for evil. Do things in such a way that everyone can see you are honest clear through.

Don't quarrel with anyone. Be at peace with everyone, just as much as possible.

Dear friends, never avenge yourselves. Leave that to God, for He has said that He will repay those who deserve it. (Don't take the law into your own hands.)

Instead, feed your enemy that is hungry. If thirsty give something to drink and you will be heaping coals of fire on their head. In other words, they will feel ashamed for what they have done to you.

Don't let evil get the upper hand but conquer evil by doing good.[22]

Obey the government, for God is the one who has put it there. Obey the laws.[23]

Pay your taxes too for government workers need to be paid so that they can keep on doing God's work, serving you.[24]

Pay everyone whatever is due them; pay your taxes and import duties gladly, obey those over you, and give honor and respect to all those to whom it is due.

Pay all your debts except the debt of love for others — never finish paying that!

If you love your neighbor as much as you love yourself you will not want to harm, or cheat, or kill, or steal from them. And you won't sin with their spouse or want what is theirs, or do anything else the Ten Commandments say is wrong.[25]

Another reason for right living is this: you know how late it is; time is running out. Wake up, for the coming of the Lord is nearer now than when we first believed.

The night is far gone, the day of His return will soon be here. So quit the evil deeds of darkness and put on the armor of right living, as we who live in the daylight should!

Be decent and true in everything you do so that all can approve your behavior.

Don't spend time in wild parties and getting drunk or in adultery and lust, or fighting, or jealousy.

But ask the Lord Jesus Christ to help you live
as you should, and don't make plans to enjoy
evil.[26]

Give a warm welcome to any person who
wants to join you, even though their faith is weak.
Don't criticize them for having different ideas
from yours.[27]

God has accepted them to be His children.
They are God's servants, not yours. They are
responsible to Him, not to you. Let Him tell them
whether they are right or wrong. And God is able
to make them do as they should.[28]

You have no right to criticize others or look
down on them. Remember, each of us will stand
personally before the Judgment Seat of God.
Yes, each of us will give account to God.

So don't criticize each other any more. Try
instead to live in such a way that you will never
make another person stumble by letting them see
you doing something they think is wrong.[29]

Don't do anything that will cause criticism
against yourself even though you know that what
you do is right. For, after all, the important thing
for us as Christians is not what we eat or drink
but stirring up goodness and peace and joy from
the Holy Spirit.

If you let Christ be Lord in these affairs,
God will be glad; and so will others. In this way
aim for harmony in the church and try to build
each other up.[30]

May God who gives patience, steadiness, and encouragement help you to live in complete harmony with each other — each with the attitude of Christ toward the other.

And then all of us can praise the Lord together with one voice, giving glory to God, the Father of our Lord Jesus Christ.

So, warmly welcome each other into the church, just as Christ has warmly welcomed you; then God will be glorified.[31]

I commit you to God, who is able to make you strong and steady in the Lord, just as the gospel says, and just as I have told you.

This is God's plan of salvation. This message is being preached everywhere, so that people all around the world will have faith in Christ and obey Him. To God, who alone is wise, be the glory forever through Jesus Christ our Lord. Amen.

Sincerely,

Paul[32]

How To Practice
The Presence Of Jesus

Since you, as a woman, have received Christ and since He has come to live in you,[33] begin to practice being conscious of His presence with you and in you. It is when He becomes a real partner with you that you begin to discover and

to experience the abundant blessings God has
planned for your life.

You yielded your life to Jesus Christ. You
can be sure that He is in you and with you.

*For you are dead, and your life is hid with
Christ in God,*[34] *for Christ is your life.*[35]   So
practice recognizing His presence in these four
distinct ways.

I
THINK what you would think if you
could actually sense the thinking process
of Christ at work within your mind.

*For to be carnally minded is death, because
the carnal mind is enmity against God for it is not
subject to the law of God, neither indeed can
be.*[36]

*Be not conformed to this world, but be trans-
formed by the renewing of your mind, that you
may prove what is that good, and acceptable and
perfect will of God.*[37]

*Be renewed in the spirit of your mind; and
put on the new creation, which is created in righteousness and true holiness.*[38]

*Let this mind be in you which was also in
Christ Jesus.*[39]

*Whatever things are true, whatever is honest,
whatever is just, whatever is of good report; if
there be any virtue, and if there be any praise,*

think on these things,[40] because we have the mind of Christ.[41]

II
SAY the things that you believe
Jesus Christ would say through you.

In the sight of God, we speak in Christ.[42]

David said, *I will speak of your testimonies. I will not be ashamed.*[43] *My tongue shall speak of your word.*[44] *My mouth shall speak the praise of the Lord.*[45]

Paul said, *It is written, I believed, and therefore I have spoken: we also believe, and therefore we speak.*[46]

You learn to believe God's word so completely that it becomes part of your vocabulary. *The word is near you, even in your mouth, and in your heart: that is the word of faith, which we preach* (or speak).[47] That is why *they overcame him* (the accuser) *by the word* (they spoke in) *their testimony.*[48]

Jesus said, *For out of the abundance of the heart the mouth speaks. A good woman out of the good treasure of the heart brings forth good things; and an evil woman out of the evil treasure of the heart brings forth evil things. But I say to you, that every idle word that you shall speak, you shall give account thereof in the day of judgment. For by your words you shall be justified, and by your words you shall be condemned.*[49]

So, *only let your conversation be as it becomes the gospel of Christ*,[50] and say only what agrees with the word of God. Be conscious of Christ's presence in everything you say. He is there. Let Him speak through you.

Let your speech be always with grace, seasoned with salt, that you may know how you should answer everyone.[51] *Use sound speech that cannot be condemned.*[52]

Jesus said, *Whoever confesses Me before people, I will confess before My Father which is in heaven.*[53]

III
GO where Jesus Christ can be welcomed as your companion.

Christ has become an integral part of your life. He says, *Lo, I am with you always.*[54] *I will dwell in you, and walk in you; and I will be your God, and you shall be My people.*[55] He loves you and cherishes your company. He says: *If you love Me and keep My words, My Father and I will come to you, and live with you.*[56]

Set your affection on things above, not on things on the earth. For you are dead, and your life is hid with Christ in God, for Christ is our life.[57]

Wherefore come out from among them, and you be separate, says the Lord, and touch not the unclean thing; and I will receive you. Having therefore these promises, dearly beloved, let us cleanse ourselves from all filthiness of the flesh and spirit, perfecting holiness in the fear of God.[58]

And you, being in time past alienated and enemies in your mind in your evil works, yet now has He reconciled in the body of His flesh through death, to present you holy and without blemish and unreproachable before Him: if so be that you continue in the faith, grounded and steadfast, are not moved away from the hope of the gospel which you heard.[59]

The Lord has promised to be a very present help in trouble[60] and to never leave you nor forsake you,[61] so only go where your Lord Jesus can accompany you and where you know He would be welcomed.

He is a friend that sticks closer than a brother or sister[62] and He wanted your companionship enough to die for your sins so He could redeem you back into His fellowship. So only go where you can be proud to invite Him along as your best friend.

IV
DO what you would do if you could see Christ alive and at work in and through you.

For the grace of God that brings salvation has appeared to all, teaching us that, denying ungodliness and worldly lusts, we should live soberly, righteously, and godly in this present world; looking for that blessed hope, and the glorious appearing of the great God and our Savior Jesus Christ; who gave Himself for us, that He might *redeem us from all iniquity, and purify to Himself a peculiar people, zealous of good works.*[63]

Be ready for every good work.[64]   *I will that you which have believed in God might be careful to maintain good works. These things are good and profitable.*[65]   *That you might show forth the praises of Him who has called you out of darkness into His marvelous light.*[66]

Be rich in good works.[67]

In all things show yourself as a pattern of good works.[68]

God is able to make all grace abound toward you; that you always having all sufficiency in all things, may abound to every good work.[69]   Paul prayed *that the child of God may be perfect, thoroughly furnished to all good works,*[70] and urged every believer to *purge yourself from (dishonorable things, so that you can)* be a vessel to *honor, sanctified, and meet for the master's use, and prepared for every good work,*[71] because He said, the seal of the foundation of the Lord is: *The Lord knows them that are His. And, let everyone that names the name of Christ depart from iniquity.*[72]

For it is written, As I live, says the Lord, every knee shall bow to me, and every tongue shall confess to God. So then every one of us shall give an account of ourselves to God.[73]

When Christ actually lives in you, as a woman, then He expresses His life through you. Your body is His temple.[74]   His mind becomes

yours.[75] His love is manifested through you.
His emotions and affections become yours.[76] All
of this happens to you as you learn to *put on the
Lord Jesus Christ.*[77] The result is that *He
works in you both to will and to do His good pleasure.*[78]

So as you grow in the Jesus-life, you train
yourself to practice His presence in you and
with you in these basic ways:

1. You think as Jesus would think through
you.

2. You speak as Jesus would speak with
your lips.

3. You go where Jesus can go with you.

4. You do as Jesus desires to do through
you.

Jesus is present in your life every moment.
Since you are His body, He wants to express
Himself and to carry out His mission of love to
others through you, as a woman. Practice letting Him do it.

Once I saw a picture of Christ with one
hand lifted toward heaven and the other reaching
down toward people in need who were gathered
about Him. That is the way it is. We learn
that just as Jesus Christ is God's bridge to humanity, we now become His bridge to them, because *in Him we live, and move, and have our being*[79] and He uses our faculties to express

Himself to people. We let Him use our hands
and bodies to achieve His purpose.

> *He has no hands but our hands*
> *To do His work today.*

> *He has no feet but our feet*
> *To lead us on His way.*

> *He has no tongue but our tongue*
> *To tell the world He died.*

> *He has no help but our help*
> *To bring them to His side.*

These vital and inspiring *Seeds Of Gold*
have now been planted in the rich soil of YOUR
life. God's incorruptible seeds guarantee a rich
harvest of His abundant blessings; they guarantee your tomorrow, enriched by His best, abound-
ing with His fullness, overflowing with His
goodness.

Re-read these *Seeds Of Gold* often and water them with your thanksgiving and your praise
to God for the rich legacy with which He has
endowed you.

God's very best will be yours.

Bible References:

1. Ro.5:2 LB
2. Ro.5:2 LB
3. Col.2:13-15 LB
4. Col.3:10 LB
5. Col.3:11 LB
6. Gal.3:28
7. Ep.2:21-22 LB
8. Col.2:8-10 LB
9. Ro.8:17 LB
10. Ro.5:2 LB
11. Ac.1:8
12. 2Co.5:20
13. 1Co.3:9
14. Ro.8:17

15. Ep.5:1
16. 1Co.12:27
17. Ep.4:15-16 LB
18. Ep.4:11-13 LB
19. Ep.4:15 LB
20. 1Pe.2:5 LB
21. Ro.12:1-2 LB
22. Ro.12:3-21 LB
23. Ro.13:1-5 LB
24. Ro.13:6 LB
25. Ro.13:7-9 LB
26. Ro.13:11-14 LB
27. Ro.14:1 LB
28. Ro.14:3-4 LB
29. Ro.14:10-13 LB
30. Ro.14:16-19 LB
31. Ro.15:5-7 LB
32. Ro.16:25-27 LB
33. Jn.14:23
34. Col.3:3
35. Col.3:4
36. Ro.8:6-7
37. Ro.12:2
38. Ep.4:23-24
39. Ph.2:5
40. Ph.4:8
41. 1Co.2:16
42. 2Co.2:17
43. Ps.119:46
44. Ps.119:172
45. Ps.145:21
46. 2Co.4:13
47. Ro.10:8
48. Re.12:11

49. Mt.12:34-37
50. Ph.1:27
51. Col.4:6
52. Tit.2:8
53. Mt.10:32
54. Mt.28:20
55. 2Co.6:16
56. Jn.14:23
57. Col.3:2-4
58. 2Co.6:17
    2Co.7:1
59. Col.1:21-23 RV
60. Ps.46:1
61. He.13:5
62. Pr.18:24
63. Tit.2:11-14
64. Tit.3:1
65. Tit.3:8
66. 1Pe.2:9
67. 1Ti.6:18
68. Tit.2:7
69. 2Co.9:8
70. 2Ti.3:17
71. 2Ti.2:20-21
72. 2Ti.2:19
73. Ro.14:11-12
74. 1Co.6:19
75. 1Co.2:16
76. 2Co.5:14
77. Ro.13:14
    Ga.3:27
78. Ph.2:13
79. Ac.17:28

Dr. Daisy arrives to set into motion another apostolic mission of gospel ministry.

WELCOME BA... . DAISY OSBOR
19th ... AUG

UGANDA WELCOMES BACK DR. DAISY

Daisy's passionate welcome by hundreds of believers is heralded by a parade through the city, to alert thousands about her upcoming Women's National Congress.

THE SON OF GOD
JESUS CHRIST

Dr. Daisy believes that the greatest achievement in life is to bring the MIRACLE gospel of Jesus to people, as she does here to a multitude in E. Africa.

Insets: She rejoices with a Moslem who was blind, a Hindu lady who was a deaf-mute since birth and an African man — all healed as she ministers to them.

Dr. Daisy's message is the good news of what Jesus Christ did for YOU when He died, in your place, on the cross.

He assumed the judgment of your sins in order to restore you to God as though you had never sinned.

No crime can be punished twice. No debt can be paid twice. He acted on your behalf. Now you have FREEDOM to become all that He has in mind for you.

VII

YOUR STEPS

TO

FREEDOM

HERE ARE 52 MIGHTY, confessions for powerful living. Here are Bible verses to confirm each fact. The greatest secret any woman can ever learn for living a successful, happy and healthy life is to discover God's thoughts and to say God's words about herself. These constitute *Your Steps To Freedom.*

It is vital for women to remember that they are *God's workmanship, created in Christ Jesus.*[1] If *any woman be in Christ, she is a new creature: old things are passed away; behold, all things are become new.*[2]

When you see yourself in Christ, and when you confess what He says about you, you will take your place as a redeemed part of the New Testament Church, marching forward in a glorious triumph of faith.

These **52** *Steps To Freedom* will help you begin to do that.

Chapter 7

YOUR STEPS TO FREEDOM

WHEN WOMEN DISCOVER their roots in God and identify with His purpose on this earth, they have begun to really live.

Your Steps To Freedom will bring you into an exhilarating and productive lifestyle based on positive faith, positive thinking, positive talking and positive acting.

What is the source of positive faith for a woman who desires God's best in life and who wants to experience personal identity, happiness and real achievement?

Faith comes by hearing the word of God.[3]

I have been inspired to share with you 52 facts — one for every week of the year — which capsulize the foundation truths I have shared with women around the world.

These basic, faith-producing facts will lift you from boring mediocrity to a fruitful partnership with God. They are the miracle stepping stones that lead you from the condemning guilt-complex of living out of harmony and out of contact with God to the success and exhilarating self-esteem which develops when you discover who you are and how you can come to God and share His lifestyle. They constitute *Your Steps To Freedom.*

As you mount these significant steps toward a more purposeful and rewarding life, you will discover a new power, new goals, and new reasons for living. You will be transformed from defeat to success, from sickness to health, from boredom to enthusiasm, from problems to solutions, from pressure to pleasure, from poverty to prosperity, from hopelessness to happiness, from despair to exciting optimism.

You will be blessed, and your family and acquaintances will be benefited too.

The Bible says: *Old things are passed away; behold, all things are become new.*[4]

Your Steps To Freedom will guide you to the abundant and the blessed life Christ wills for you — to real *Life For Women.* These steps will become the foundation stones on which you build your new life.

Review them often. Rehearse them in prayer. Memorize them. Recite them in family worship. Recount them to relatives and to friends. Enumerate them. They will keep infusing you with God's wonderful *Life For Women* as you keep them in your heart and on your lips.

Anyone who sets out to climb these *Steps To Freedom* will discover, sooner or later, a very real enemy who desperately wants to block your progress and to keep you on a lower, limited level of life. The Bible calls this enemy Satan and mentions him at least 175 times by such names as *Lucifer,*[5] *the devil,*[6] *Satan,*[7] *the adversary,*[8] *the god of this world,*[9] *the enemy,*[10] *the tempter,*[11] *the wicked one,*[12] *the ruler of darkness,*[13] *the murderer,*[14] and by other names.

You will meet him in his most subtle form as *the accuser.*[15]

So when you are discouraged, or tempted to doubt your experience with God, rehearse these fifty-two facts of the Jesus *Life For Women.*

That is the effective way to *resist the devil,* and James said *he will flee from you.*[16]

The apostle John said, *They overcame* (Satan) *by the word of their testimony;*[17] and Jesus defeated every temptation of Satan by saying, *It is written,*[18] then by quoting a scripture.

When the accuser tempts you, rehearse these facts and confess these scriptures and it will happen to you as it did to Jesus: *Then the devil left Him, and, behold, angels came and ministered to Him.*[19]

So, here are *Your Steps To Freedom.* Learn these facts and make these verses your confession, as a woman. (I have personalized the Bible quotations to help you to identify with them in your life.):

READ THESE FACTS AND SCRIPTURES OUT LOUD.

1. I was unsaved before I received Christ.

For I have sinned, and come short of the glory of God.[20]

2. I was guilty before God, under the penalty of death.

For the wages of (my) *sin is death.*[21]

3. But God loved me too much to see me perish.

He is not willing that I should perish, but that I should come to repentance.[22]

4. God offered His best to prove His love to me.

God so loved the world (including **me**) *that He gave His only begotten Son, that when I believe in Him, I shall not perish, but have everlasting life.*[23]

5. Christ was God's gift and He died for me.

But God commends His love toward me, in that while I was yet a sinner, Christ died for me.[24]

6. I realize that my sins separated me from God.

My iniquities have separated between me and my God, and my sins have hid His face from me.[25]

7. Knowing that my sins cost God His Son, and Jesus His life and blood, I repent of them.

I sorrowed to repentance; for godly sorrow works repentance to salvation[26] *and* I know that *except I repent, I shall perish.*[27]

8. I confess my sins to Him and I believe I am cleansed.

If I confess my sins, He is faithful and just to forgive me of my sins, and to cleanse me from all unrighteousness.[28]

9. I recognize Jesus at the door of my heart. I open it and He comes in.

Behold, I stand at the door, and knock: if you hear My voice, and open the door, I will come in and will sup with you and you with me[29] (meaning to dine and have fellowship together).

10. I receive Jesus and I now become God's child.

As I receive Jesus Christ, He gives me power to become a child of God, even to me because I believe on His name.[30]

11. I become a new creature.

If I am in Christ, I am a new creature: old things are passed away; behold, all things are become new.[31]

12. I know I am born again because I do receive Christ in my life.

Jesus said, *I must be born again*[32] *and when I received Christ, He gives me power to become*

God's child.[33] I was *born, not of blood, nor of
the will of the flesh, nor of the will of a human
being, but of God,*[34] *by the word of God which
lives and abides forever.*[35]

13. I believe the powerful message of the
gospel that saves me.

*The gospel is the power of God to salvation to
everyone* (including me) *that believes.*[36]

14. I believe on the name of Jesus Christ
because of the record of the Gospels.

*These are written, that I might believe that
Jesus is the Christ, the Son of God; and that believing I might have life through His name.*[37]

15. I call on His name and am saved.

Whoever (including me) *shall call upon the
name of the Lord shall be saved.*[38]

16. I recognize that Jesus is my only way
to God.

*He said, I am the way, the truth and the life:
no one comes to the Father but by me.*[39] *There is
one God, and one mediator between God and me,
the man Christ Jesus.*[40]

17. I know there is salvation in none other.

*Neither is there salvation in any other: for
there is none other name under heaven given
whereby I must be saved.*[41]

18. I put my faith in Jesus as Savior.

For by grace am I saved through faith; and that not of myself: it is the gift of God: not of works, lest I should boast.[42]

19. I believe that the Lord comes into my life.

The Lord Almighty says, I will dwell in you, and walk in you; and I will be your God, and you shall be My child. I will be a Father to you, and you shall be My son or daughter.[43]

20. I do not trust in any good works or self-righteousness to be saved.

My righteousness is like filthy rags.[44] *My salvation was not of works, lest I should boast.*[45]

21. I am saved only by God's mercy.

Not by works of righteousness which I have done, but according to His mercy He saved me, by the washing of regeneration, and renewing of the Holy Ghost; Which He shed on me abundantly through Jesus Christ our Savior; That being justified by His grace, I should be made an heir according to the hope of eternal life.[46]

22. I know Christ's death justifies me before God.

Being justified by faith, I have peace with God through my Lord Jesus Christ.[47]

23. I know His blood remits my sins forever.

Christ said, *This is My blood which is shed
for you for the remission of sins.*[48]   *Being justified by His blood, I shall be saved from wrath
through Him.*[49]

24. I know I am cleansed from sin.

Christ *loved me, and washed me from my
sins in His own blood;*[50]   *In whom I have redemption through His blood, even the forgiveness
of sins.*[51]

25. I know my sins are put away and forgotten.

*Behold the Lamb of God, which takes away
the sin of the world.*[52]   *He has removed my
transgressions from me as far as the east is from
the west*[53] *so that my sins and iniquities will He
remember no more.*[54]

26. I know my sins were paid for by
Christ's death.

*Who His own self bore my sins in His own
body on the tree, that I, being dead to sins, should
live to righteousness.*[55]   *He was wounded for my
transgressions. He was bruised for my iniquities:
the chastisement of my peace was upon Him.*[56]

27.   With my sins punished and washed
away, I know they can never condemn me again.

There is therefore now no condemnation to me, because I am in Christ Jesus.[57] *For God made Him who knew no sin, to be sin for me; that I might be made the righteousness of God in Christ*[58] *and where remission is, there is no more offering for sin*[59] so that now nothing *shall separate me from the love of Christ.*[60]

28. I know when I accept Christ that I receive His life.

Those (including me) *that have the Son, have life.*[61] Christ said, *They that hear My word, and believe on Him that sent Me, have everlasting life, and shall not come into condemnation, but are passed from death to life.*[62] *And this is life eternal, that I might know the only true God, and Jesus Christ whom He has sent.*[63]

29. I know Satan will accuse me.

He is the accuser which accuses me before my God day and night[64] just like he accused Job.[65]

30. I am not ignorant of His works.

Lest Satan should get an advantage of me: for I am not ignorant of His devices.[66] For I know that he *comes to steal, and to kill, and to destroy.*[67]

31. I know how Jesus overcame him.

But Jesus answered and said, it is written.[68] *Then the devil left Him, and, behold, angels came and ministered to Him.*[69]

32. I know Jesus proved that Satan could not win.

Christ was in all points tempted like I am, yet without sin. I can therefore come boldly to the throne of grace, that I may obtain mercy, and find grace to help in time of need.[70]

33. I know He faithfully helps me in temptation.

No temptation has taken me but such as is common to people: but God is faithful, who will not suffer me to be tempted above that I am able; but will with the temptation also make a way to escape, that I may be able to bear it.[71]

34. I know that there are two weapons Satan can never resist.

And I overcome him (the devil who accuses me before God day and night) *by the blood of the Lamb, and by the word of my testimony.*[72]

35. I know Satan cannot win over my faith.

I shall be sober and vigilant; because my adversary the devil, as a roaring lion, walks about, seeking whom he may devour: Whom I resist steadfast in the faith.[73] *I resist the devil, and he flees from me. I draw near to God, and He draws near to me;*[74] *I who am the begotten of God keep myself, and that wicked one touches me not.*[75]

36. I know my faith is the victory.

For whoever (including me) *is born of God overcomes the world: and this is the victory that overcomes the world, even my faith.*[76]

37. I know not to love the world but to do God's will.

Love not the world, neither the things that are in the world. If anyone loves the world, the love of the Father is not in them. For all that is in the world, the lust of the flesh, and the lust of the eyes, and the pride of life, is not of the Father, but is of the world. And the world passes away, and the lust thereof; but those who do the will of God live for ever.[77]

38. I know Christ came to defeat my enemy.

For this purpose the Son of God was manifested, that He might destroy the works of the devil.[78]

39. I know Satan is no match for Christ in me.

Christ in me, the hope of glory.[79] God says, *I will dwell in you and walk in you.*[80] *I am of God, and I have overcome, because greater is He that is in me than he that is in the world.*[81]

40. I know my new life source is the Lord Jesus Christ.

I am crucified with Christ: nevertheless I live; yet not I, but Christ lives in me: and the life which I now live in the flesh I live by the faith of the Son of God, who loved me, and gave Himself for me.[82]

41. I know my new life has divine purpose.

My steps are ordered by the Lord and God delights in my way. Though I fall, I shall not be utterly cast down: for the Lord upholds me with His hand.[83]

42. I know God sees me and hears me.

For the eyes of the Lord are over the righteous and His ears are open to their prayers.[84]

43. I know He invites me to call on Him.

God says, *Call to me, and I will answer you.*[85] He says, *If I ask, it shall be given me; if I seek, I shall find; if I knock, it shall be opened to me. For everyone* (including me) *who asks receives.*[86]

44. I know when I pray that He answers.

Christ promises, *Whatever things I desire, when I pray, believe that I receive them, and I shall have them;*[87] *and whatever I shall ask in Christ's name, that will He do, that the Father may be glorified in the Son.*[88]

45.   I know that I belong to God's royal family.

I am a chosen generation, a royal priesthood, an holy nation, a peculiar people; that I should show forth the praises of Him who has called me out of darkness into His marvelous light.[89]

46. I know that all that Christ has now belongs to me.

For all who are led by the spirit of God are children of God. And so I should not be like a cringing, fearful slave, but I should behave like God's very own child, adopted into the bosom of His family, and calling Him, Father, Father. For His Holy Spirit speaks to me deep in my heart, and tells me that I really am God's child. And since I am His child, I will share His treasures — for all that God gives to His Son Jesus is now mine too.[90]

47. I know I have His life in my flesh now.

That the life of Jesus might be made manifest in my mortal flesh,[91] *for my body is the temple of the Holy Ghost.*[92]

48. I know I never need to live in want again.

My God shall supply all my need according to His riches in glory by Christ Jesus,[93] *for no good thing will He withhold from me as I walk uprightly.*[94]

49. I no longer fear diseases and plagues.

There shall no evil befall me, neither shall any plague come near my dwelling,[95] *because it is the Lord who heals me.*[96] Jesus *took my in-*

firmities and bore *my* sicknesses[97] and *with His stripes I am healed.*[98]

50.   I am no longer oppressed by problems.

Casting all my care upon Him; for He cares for me.[99]

51.   I know I am a winner.

If God be for me, who can be against me?[100] *No, in all these things I am more than a conqueror through Him that loved me.*[101]   *He which has begun a good work in me will perform it until the day of Jesus Christ.*[102]   *Faithful is He that calls me, who also will do it.*[103]

52.   I know Christ is with me to the end.

For He has said, I will never leave you, nor forsake you. So that I may boldly say, The Lord is my helper, and I will not fear what any person shall do to me,[104] *and, Christ says, lo, I am with you always, even to the end of the world.*[105]

Value What You Say

Now, you have just read 52 positive confessions of faith in God's word.   You as a woman, have made His word the authority in your life.

Few people realize it but women always sink or rise to the level of their words — the same as men do.   Solomon said, *You are snared with the words of your mouth, you are taken (captive) with the words of your mouth.*[106]

Words are energizers. They are power-filled. If you talk weakness, sickness, failure, inadequacy or fear, your words are the seeds by which those influences are planted in your life, and you grow them in you.

If you talk salvation, health, happiness, prosperity and success, by your own words you are planting those good seeds in your life and you will inevitably reap their harvest.

Re-read those 52 confessions. Learn the Bible verses concerning each fact. The greatest secret you can ever learn for living a successful, happy and healthy life as a woman, is to learn to think God's thoughts and to say God's words. You will discover that these are really *Your Steps To Freedom.*

Then discipline yourself to act according to God's word, because without corresponding action, your faith is dead. *Be doers of the word, and not hearers only, deceiving your own selves.*[107]

Remember that *Jesus Christ has delivered you from the power of darkness, and has translated you into the kingdom of His dear Son: in whom you have redemption through His blood, even the forgiveness of sins.*[108]

This means that Satan's dominion over you as a redeemed woman, has ended, and Jesus' dominion has begun.

Disease and sickness, weakness and failure, can no longer rule over you. You are redeemed. You are saved.

As Christian women embrace biblical verses like the ones I am including here, a new breed of women-believers is birthed in the church.

For example, this verse has powerful meaning for a believing woman:

Fear not; for I am with you: be not dismayed; for I am your God: I will strengthen you; yes, I will help you; yes, I will uphold you with the right hand of my righteousness.[109]

If God be for us (as women), *who can be against us?*[110]

You are of God, (women), *and have overcome them: because greater is He that is in you, than he that is in the world.*[111]

The Lord is my light and my salvation; whom shall I fear?

The Lord is the strength of my life; of whom shall I be afraid?[112]

He is your salvation and deliverance from every demeaning trap that the enemy sets for you.

You have no fear, because God is on your side.

As women, we are to confess what we are in Christ: that we are redeemed, that our redemption is an actual fact, that we are delivered out of the dominion and authority of Satan. That is confessing *Life For Women.*

We confess that we as women, are actually new creatures, recreated in Christ Jesus; that we are *partakers of His divine nature;*[113] that sickness, disease, fear, infirmities and subjugation are things of the past for us.

Our language amazes our friends. It seems absurd and presumptuous to them, but to us it is simply stating facts which are written in the word; it is the language of God's royal daughters.

It is vital for women to remember that we are His (God's) *workmanship, created in Christ Jesus.*[114] Through Jesus Christ, God made us what we are — a new creation. *If anyone be in Christ she or he is a new creature: old things are passed away; behold, all things are become new.*[115]

All Jesus did was for us. He had no need to conquer Satan for Himself. He did it for us. He had no sins of His own to carry away. He had no sin until He took our sins. He did this for us as women.

He had no need to put away sickness for Himself. He had no sickness until He was made sick for us. He did this for us as women.

All That Jesus Did Was For Us

We were captives, but Christ has freed us from captivity.

We were cursed by sin, but Christ, our Redeemer, has freed us from that curse and loosed us from its dominion.

We were weak, but the Lord has become our strength. Now we are strong.

We were bound and imprisoned, but Christ has freed us from slavery.

We were sick, but Christ bore our sicknesses and carried them away; now with *His stripes we are healed.*

We were lost, but now we are (re)created in Christ. We are members of Him, and He is in us.

As a woman believer, embrace and confess these facts in a positive way: *Christ lives in ME.*[116] *Christ dwells in MY heart by faith.*[117] *Christ in ME, the hope of glory.*[118] *Christ ... is MY life.*[119] *But of Him am I in Christ Jesus.*[120] *Jesus Christ is in ME.*[121]

When any believing woman begins to see herself in Christ, and then begins to confess that, instead of talking about her inferiority, lack, inability, and sickness, she becomes an irresistible member of the body of Christ — a royal daughter in God's family, with all of the rights and privileges of any member of His divine household.

Women who are aware of their legal standing in God take their places as redeemed members of the New Testament church, marching forward in this glorious triumph of faith.

Remember, Satan is eternally defeated, and God's word is always triumphant when it is believed and spoken by any woman believer.

During the great temptation in the wilderness, the only weapon Jesus used was the word of God, and it always conquers!

That is why I have published these 52 facts (or confessions) for women, based on God's word, so that you can learn them. Build your life on these facts. Speak them in times of testing, and Satan will leave you as he left Jesus, when he hears God's word coming from your lips.

And remember to expect angels to come and to minister to you, as they came and ministered to Christ.[122]

Bible References: Page 180

Dr. Daisy conducts National Women's Miracle Day at Kampala, Uganda with over 200,000 women in attendance — besides men and children.

Dr. Daisy teaches thousands of African women at National Women's Ministry Seminar in Kenya's Nyanza province.

Dr. Daisy conducts a National Women's Conference at Accra, Ghana, meets the Head of State and prophesies the strategic changes marking the nation's re-birth.

Bible References:

1. Ep.2:10
2. 2Co.5:17
3. Ro.10:17
4. 2Co.5:17
5. Is.14:12-14
6. Mt.4:1
   Ep.6:11
7. Re.12:9
8. 1Pe.5:8
9. 2Co.4:4
10. Mt.13:39
11. Mt.4:3
12. Mt.13:19
13. Ep.6:12
14. Jn.8:44
15. Re.12:10
16. Ja.4:7
17. Re.12:11
18. Mt.4:4,7,10
19. Mt.4:11
20. Ro.3:23
21. Ro.6:23
22. 2Pe.3:9
23. Jn.3:16
24. Ro.5:8
25. Is.59:2
26. 2Co.7:9-10
27. Lu.13:3
28. 1Jn.1:9
29. Re.3:20
30. Jn.1:12
31. 2Co.5:17
32. Jn.3:7
33. Jn.1:12
34. Jn.1:13
35. 1Pe.1:23
36. Ro.1:16
37. Jn.20:31
38. Ro.10:13
39. Jn.14:6
40. 1Ti.2:5
41. Ac.4:12

42. Ep.2:8-9
43. 2Co.6:16,18
44. Is.64:6
45. Ep.2:9
46. Tit.3:5-7
47. Ro.5:1
48. Mt.26:28
49. Ro.5:9
50. Re.1:5
51. Col.1:14
52. Jn.1:29
53. Ps.103:12
54. He.10:17
55. 1Pe.2:24
56. Is.53:5
57. Ro.8:1
58. 2Co.5:21
59. He.10:18
60. Ro.8:35
61. 1Jn.5:12
62. Jn.5:24
63. Jn.17:3
64. Re.12:10
65. Job1:6-12
66. 2Co.2:11
67. Jn.10:10
68. Mt.4:4,7,10
69. Mt.4:11
70. He.4:15-16
71. 1Co.10:13
72. Re.12:11
73. 1Pe.5:8-9
74. Ja.4:7-8
75. 1Jn.5:18
76. 1Jn.5:4
77. 1Jn.2:15-17
78. 1Jn.3:8
79. Col.1:27
80. 2Co.6:16,18
81. 1Jn.4:4
82. Ga.2:20
83. Ps.37:23-24

84. 1Pe.3:12
85. Je.33:3
86. Lu.11:9-10
87. Mk.11:24
88. Jn.14:13
89. 1Pe.2:9
90. Ro.8:14-17 LB
91. 2Co.4:11
92. 1Co.6:19
    1Co.3:16-17
93. Ph.4:19
94. Ps.84:11
95. Ps.91:10
96. Ex.15:26
97. Mt.8:17
98. Is.53:5
    1Pe.2:24
99. 1Pe.5:7
100. Ro.8:31
101. Ro.8:37
102. Ph.1:6
103. 1Th.5:24
104. He.13:5-6
105. Mt.28:20
106. Pr.6:2
107. Ja.1:22
108. Col.1:13-14
109. Is.41:10
110. Ro.8:31
111. 1Jn.4:4
112. Ps.27:1
113. 2Pe.1:4
114. Ep.2:10
115. 2Co.5:17
116. Ga.2:20
117. Ep.3:17
118. Col.1:27
119. Col.3:4
120. 1Co.1:30
121. 2Co.13:5
122. Mt.4:11

VIII

LIVING

BY

LOVING

WHETHER ON THE busy streets of Paris, New York or Bogota; whether in village towns of the Philippines, India, China or Africa, women's search for God is written on their faces, expressed in the way they walk, reflected in their spirits.

Plagued by inner fears and guilts, women permit their lives to be eroded by psychological traumas which poison their systems, engendering disease and deterioration.

I have watched the light turn on in the faces of tens of thousands of women when they realized how much God values them and that He wills success, health, happiness and abundance in their lives.

Real *Life* is found in real *Love.* Grasp this and you will discover the true happiness of *Living By Loving.*

Chapter 8

LIVING BY LOVING

I WISH THE whole world could know how good God is.

The Lord is gracious and full of compassion.[1] Jesus was everywhere *moved with compassion.*[2] *His compassions fail not.*[3]

Thirty-four times in the Book of Psalms, the Bible says, *His mercy endures forever.*

For You, Lord, are good, and ready to forgive; and plenteous in mercy to all them that call upon you.[4]

God says, *I will rejoice over you to do you good ... with my whole heart and with my whole soul.*[5] God has a very big heart and soul, and it all rejoices over you and me to do us good.

Many people think of God as some sort of dominating master who lords it over people with a whip in His hand to afflict and punish His children with sickness, suffering and poverty. This is not true.

God created you and me for His wonderful lifestyle and He wants us to enjoy His blessings of happiness, health, success and prosperity. That is His will for you and for me today.

God created woman in His own image, the same as He did man. Therefore, human beings (both men and women) instinctively search for God's lifestyle; whether they admit it and are conscious of it or not.

Since I am a woman, I call it a search for *Life For Women.*

When The Light Turns On

Around the world, whether on the busy streets of Paris, New York or Bogota; whether in village towns of the Philippines, India, China or Africa, instinctive search is for a living God. It is written all over theirs faces. It is expressed in the way they walk. It is reflected in their spirits. They would give anything on earth to know that God is real, and that they could find some approach to Him. To imagine that such a God, if real and living, is interested in them individually seems beyond their imagination.

I have watched the light turn on in the faces of tens of thousands of women (and of men) when they realized that God loves them, that He is not angry at them, that He cares for each detail of their lives. It can happen to you as a woman, while reading this book.

The truth of the matter is that God wants a woman's life to be fulfilled and successful in the same way that He does for any man. He wants women to enjoy happiness and to develop their finest talents and capabilities. A woman's potential is God-given and limitless. God has the same pleasure in seeing women blossom and succeed as any good parent experiences when their child excels.

God is not a destroying deity who sends disease and pain.[6] He does not want poverty and lack in your life. He has plenty, and it is for you to enjoy.[7]

God is never pleased by needless suffering, poverty, sickness and failure.

Women, plagued by inner fears and guilts, poison their own systems and engender within themselves disease and deterioration. Young and old alike, they permit their lives to be eroded by the psychological traumas and chemical poison of hatred, jealousy, envy and greed.

Their lack of faith in God, in others, and in themselves, makes them crumble and degenerate into unproductive or unfulfilled lives.

Capable and talented women often allow their lives to be wasted or limited because of the influence of religion and of society upon the female person. The plague of poverty curses millions of capable and talented women who live in a world of abundance, but who have never been encouraged (or allowed) to put their own talents and capabilities into creative action.

Women who should be physically vibrant and healthy, in service to God and to others, deteriorate by inactivity, disease and pain, never having tasted the exuberating thrill or never having sensed the energizing force of life that comes from enterprising achievement.

The gnawing, noxious cancers of negativism, resentment, remorse and despair poison the life-stream of thousands of potentially creative women who could have given to their world incalculable wealth.

These are the reasons I have published this book about *Life For Women.*

God created womankind with the same creative and enterprising talents that He gave to men, but religion and culture have repressed those abilities. But God has never given up on His dream for women.

His love and mercy, His power and healing, His miracle presence in your life can bring an end to disease, defeat, poverty and despair in women.

He is good and He wills only good for women.

He is love and He yearns for women to share that love.

He is life and wants to pour that life into women.

He carries no whip and He wills no doom.

He created you in His image, so that makes you His kind of being.

She Looked Like An Angel

God offers to women an abundant and miracle lifestyle. Jesus said, *I am come that you might have life, and that you might have it more abundantly.*[8] He spoke that to women who followed Him, the same as to men.

In one of our teaching crusades abroad, a prostitute who was dying of cancer was hauled to our meeting in an old wheelbarrow. Some Christians found her wasting away, languishing on a straw mat on the ground, in a tiny adobe hut where she had been abandoned to die.

When they told her about the crusade and offered to take her there, she was overwhelmed by their kindness. At first she objected because she was sure there was no hope for her ruined life. She had spent her years in prostitution and felt guilty and ashamed.

The Christians convinced her that *God had not sent His Son to the world to condemn the world; but that the world through Him might be saved.*[9] They assured her of God's love for her.

They placed pillows in the old wheelbarrow and hauled her to the meeting. Her emaciated body resembled a sallow skin-covered skeleton, except for her swollen cancer-ridden abdomen.

Lying there in the wheelbarrow under the open sky, she listened to our teaching about the new life of Jesus Christ and how anyone can receive Him into their life by faith.

The Life-Giving Power Of Love

I remember well the subject we addressed that night. It was about receiving Christ and about the miracle that takes place when this new life is accepted by faith.

We emphasized how Jesus died on the cross in our name, to suffer the judgment of our sins so that we could be restored to God as though we had never sinned. We stressed the fact that when we believe in His love and accept what He accomplished for us, that we can receive Him into our lives and that when He comes to live in us, His life transforms us and creates in us a new person; that His life heals our sicknesses and regenerates us spiritually, mentally and physically.

When we finished the teaching and led the crowd of some 35,000 people in prayer to accept Christ, that woman came to understand that Jesus had already assumed all judgment for all of her sins. He had done it because God valued her, just as she was. She repeated the prayer with us.

The realization of God's immeasurable love dawned upon her as she prayed to Him and received Him into her heart. She understood that since Christ bore all punishment for her sins, she was exonerated, acquitted, absolved from her sins and that she was no longer guilty.

She accepted her pardon and forgiveness and received Jesus Christ into her life by faith. His new life was imparted to her old nature

and she was regenerated by the incomprehensible
power of the life and love of Jesus Christ.
She discovered the power of God's love in action.

Lying there, weeping for joy, overflowing
with peace and thanksgiving, she looked up at
her friends, reached out her bony arms to their
strong hands and was raised up on her feet for
the first time in months.

The Cancer Disappeared

As they wept and thanked God together, the
dear woman was so overcome with joy and peace
in her soul that she forgot about her large can-
cerous tumor. In a few moments, she suddenly
realized that it had disappeared and that her legs
and arms had become strong.

She was not only forgiven of her sins and
restored to dignity in God's family; she was
also miraculously cured of the cancer.

She marched through the press of people,
and up the steps of the platform. I can remember her standing there with tears streaming
down her cheeks, with those bony arms raised
toward heaven. Her upturned face looked like
that of an angel.

Her entire lifestyle was changed. *Old things
were passed away; all things had become new.*[10]

She became a faithful and devoted follower
of Christ and consecrated her life to helping
other people to know about God's love.

What that woman received from God is the life and vigor, the happiness and health which Jesus Christ came to share with you and every woman who believes the Gospel. That is what I call real authentic *Life For Women.*

Your Way To Real Life

God's plan for you, just like His original dream, is based on faith in His integrity, confidence and trust in His word. His only condition for you is that you honor and trust what He says. In turn, He wants to honor and to trust you.

At the cost of giving His own Son, God proved forever the integrity of His word.

The Bible asks: *God promises, and does He not perform? Does He not carry out His word?*[11]

Here is what I mean.

God loved you and found a legal way to absolve you from every sin you ever committed.

Jesus came on a love mission to show you God's original dream for you. He lived a beautiful, inspiring life, without ever dishonoring God or questioning the integrity of His word.

Having lived without sin, He gave His life for you and died in your name, under the penalty of your sins, as your substitute. He bore all legal judgment that was against you.

Relate To God Through Christ And Live

How do you as a woman, relate to what He did for you? How does it affect you in your problems and needs right now? What should you do about it?

The Bible says, *Whoever believes in Jesus Christ shall not perish* (or suffer the wages of sin which is death), *but have eternal life.*[12]

God's love is offered to every woman who chooses to believe in His love. You are free to believe what He has said in the Bible and to accept His words as true.

Or you are free not to believe it. You have the personal right to carry on as you are, and to remain subject to disease, loneliness, inferiority and condemnation.

God's plan for you depends on your willingness to understand and to believe that Jesus Christ died in your name, as your personal substitute, in your own place.

This is the key that unlocks God's blessings for you.

This involves your will.

You have the right of choice. You are free to accept the validity of what Christ did on your behalf, or to reject it as superstition or as irrelevant or as insignificant.

Trust The Plan That Works

God's love depends upon your faith, just like He required Adam and Eve to trust His integrity.

Here are some great statements to encourage you to trust in the Lord:

Anyone (that includes every woman) *who believes in Jesus Christ is not judged at all.*[13]

All who trust God's Son to save them have eternal life.[14]

What specifically are you as a woman, to trust or believe?

1.   That Jesus was sinless and perfect;

2.   That He died in your name, on your behalf and bore the judgment you should have borne;

3.   That He did it because God loves you and wants to live with you;

4.   That God values you so much that He paid this infinite price to make that possible.

5.   That Jesus paid that price to restore you to God even before you knew you were estranged from Him. It was His idea to redeem you to Himself — not your idea.

Facts For Every Woman

These remarkable facts are what constitute God's plan for women.

Jesus Christ suffered the penalty of every woman's sins so that you can be saved from death and live eternally as He planned for you.

He suffered the consequences of every woman's sins so that you can be forever absolved from guilt, condemnation or judgment.

He took upon Himself every woman's pains, infirmities and sicknesses, so that you can be free of them and live in health and enjoy longevity.

He bore every woman's insecurity, shame, inferiority and loneliness, so that you can live in fellowship and friendship with God again.

He died so that every woman can live.

He assumed every woman's guilt so that you can receive His righteousness.

God took the sinless Christ and poured into Him your sins. Then, in exchange, He pours God's goodness into you.[15]

The record of every woman's sins was credited to Christ's account. Then He assumed every woman's guilt and bore the judgment you deserved, in your name.

In exchange, His righteousness was credited to every woman's account and you were declared righteous in God's eyes forever.

God Values You And Needs You

The greatest idea that God has ever shared with women is His idea that they are valuable to Him and that He loves them so much that He has paid an incredible price for your happiness, health and success in life.

The love of God was proven toward us, because He sent His only begotten Son into the world that we might have life through Him.[16]

He wants every woman to live His kind of life — happy, productive, abundant, healthy.

The Bible says, *Herein is love, not that we loved God but that He loved us and sent His Son to be the sacrifice for our sins.*[17]

God Can Now Live In You

You see, the miracle of the gospel is that women are restored to God by His love, not by anything we could ever do. As soon as we believe that, God can come back in us and live in us and through us like He originally planned, and carry out His work among people through us as His women ambassadors.

When Jesus, God's Son came and lived on this earth, He showed the goodness, kindness and compassion of God at work among people. When God comes home to live in us like He lived in Christ, He wants to continue doing the same things through us as women, as He did through Jesus, because we are restored to Him and now He can live in us.

When women learn to believe in God's love that releases His dynamic love power in them to reach out and to help lift their world.

When God's love works in you and through you as a woman, that is God's power at work in you and through you. I call it real *Life For Women*, or I call it *Living By Loving*.

When any woman reaches out her hand to a fallen person and picks someone up, that is God's hand in action. The power of God's love is being extended through that woman. It is His miracle power — the miracle of love in action. There is no creative force in this world like the power of God's love at work in and through a human person who represents Jesus among people.

We Can Live Because We Love

Women must remember that God is love. Since women were created by God, each woman is the product of love. Women are the off-spring of love. No wonder it is natural for us to love. It is unnatural for us not to love.

Our nervous system cannot sustain hate. It will produce chemical poison in our system and cause disease to invade our physical body and kill us prematurely.

Since Jesus Christ paid the full price for every woman's sins, if you believe that He did it for you and in your name, that means you are legally free from all guilt, and nothing you have ever done can now separate you from God. You are restored to a position of friendship and rapport with Him. He is love. His emotions can now flow through you again.

The Love Plan Took Root In Us

That is what happened to my husband and me so many years ago when we welcomed Christ into our lives. As young people we were fortunate enough to hear about God's redemptive plan and we believed in it.

As a result, we felt that since Jesus had done such wonderful things for us, our lives could be given to tell others about Him.

When we were married at the young ages of seventeen and eighteen, we dedicated ourselves to sharing the gospel of Jesus with other people. When we were only twenty and twenty one years old, we took our ten-month-old son and sailed to the other side of the world to share the gospel in India, to share Christ and His love with the Moslems and the Hindus.

Now for more than four decades, in over seventy different nations, we have travelled and proclaimed the Gospel out in open stadiums or parks or fields, out where scores of thousands of people of all religions can feel free to assemble without intimidation, and hear the teachings of Jesus Christ.

Perhaps we have taught the good news, face-to-face, to more millions of unchurched people than any other couple who ever lived. It is possible that we have seen more great healing miracles among the masses of unchurched people around the world, than any other couple on earth — not because our faith is any greater, but simply because we have ministered to so many multitudes, in so many areas of the world, for so many years.

Discovering Self-Worth

God's love works through us to reach people. That is His idea for us. We love people. We want to help them. God values them and needs them. We want them to know of His love and esteem for them. We know that if they discover how much God values them, they will begin to discover self-value and they will stop destroying and condemning and hating themselves and others.

We know that if people stop deprecating themselves, they will stop deprecating others. If they stop their self-destruction they will stop destroying others.

I think there is no life as great as to see people who are lonely, insecure, fearful, unloved, uncared for, forgotten or neglected, and to be able to give them the message of God's love that motivates them to stand up, to straighten their shoulders, to lift their heads and to walk with a long stride, realizing that they count with God. To help give dignity to human persons is the ultimate in fulfillment. That is why I can-

not comprehend a theology or an ecclesiastic
dogma or tradition that demeans or represses or
subjugates or devalues women whom God Himself has created in His own divine image and
likeness.

To lift people and to help them discover the
rich and purposeful life God created them for,
to help them discover that God loves them, that
Jesus gave His life for them; *to lift beggars out
of the dunghill and to set them on high with God,*[18]
as the Bible says, is the greatest life on earth.
That is the power of God's love in action and
He imparts that power to every woman who believes on Him and who receives Christ. Every
woman can go forth with that power, as Christ's
witness and co-worker, exactly the same as any
man can. That is real *Life For Women.*

You see, that is what God has done for us,
and that is what He now does through us as we
share His love with others.

That is the reason this book is in your
hands as a woman. God is saying to each woman:

*I love you. I value you. The price I paid
for you proves what I think you are worth.*

*Believe in my love and let me restore to you
the riches, the happiness, the health and the
abundance I created for you.*

*Then I will be able to reach out to others
through you, and in that way, your life will fulfill
its divine purpose as you discover the happiness*

of becoming my friend and partner in helping others.

The Buddhist Found The Way

I can assure you that the truths of this book work for women the same as they do for men. I am sure that you are experiencing a new understanding of your place, as a woman, in God's plan.

We have watched thousands of Moslems, Buddhists, Shintoists, Hindus, fetish-worshipers, atheists and nominal Christians turn to Jesus Christ and receive Him into their hearts and become radiant new creatures as soon as they came to understand the simple but powerful facts of the gospel that you are now discovering.

No Difference In People

I can tell you that people are basically the same worldwide. They commit the same sins, experience the same needs, sense the same guilt, suffer the same diseases and instinctively search for the same peace, regardless of race, sex, color, nationality or background.

When people really understand the gospel, they react with the same overwhelming satisfaction. I have watched thousands of stoic and traditionally calm American Indians, Eskimos and Japanese people experience the wonder of God's new life. The effect upon them is no different than what happened to people in Bible days.

We have watched hundreds of mature Moslems experience this miracle in a single night and react the same as one might expect to see in the West.

We have observed placid and poised Buddhists break into tears of gratitude as they believed on Jesus Christ and discovered His love for them.

We have proven what the Bible says: *For there is no difference ... the same Lord over all is rich unto all who call on Him, for whoever shall call on the name of the Lord shall be saved.*[19]

At 74, She Heard The Gospel

During our crusade in southern Thailand, a 74 year old Buddhist nun attended. She was placed in the temple when she was only a girl and had consecrated her life to serve the temple.

Our public crusade was conducted out under the shade of a huge coconut palm grove. The sound from our loud speakers reached her ears.

She slipped away from the temple and bought a piece of cloth in the market place with which she could conceal her identity, since her only clothing was an white nun's habit.

She stood in a shadowy area at the edge of the field to avoid recognition.

That night my husband, T.L. Osborn spoke the good news of what Jesus did on the cross for everyone. He quoted various scriptures which explained how humanity had sinned, how God loved us and valued us so much that He gave His Son for us, how Jesus bore the sin and guilt and condemnation that we deserved and how He died in our place, was buried and then rose from the dead, and that He lives today and wants to come into our lives in order to share God's abundant life, peace, forgiveness, health and blessing with us.

That old woman had never heard those gospel facts in all of her life.

The Beautiful Report

She came to our cottage the next day. We sat for two hours out under those beautiful palm trees as she tried to tell us, through the interpreter, what had happened.

Her eyes glistened like a young maiden as she explained how she had received Jesus Christ and had been made new inside.

She said, *All of my life, I searched for peace. The only thing I knew to do was to work hard in the temple and to serve the priests every way possible.*

I soon learned that everyone in the temple was searching for the same peace that I sought, but that we were all unsatisfied. The others were as unhappy as I was.

I often wondered if there was anything else I could do to find peace in my heart. Many nights, I wept for hours in the darkness when no one could see me. I felt guilt but I knew no way to find peace.

Just look at me. I am 74 years old. Now, I have finally discovered the peace I had sought all of my life.

The first time I listened to you, Dr. Osborn, when you talked about God loving me and sending His Son to die on the cross for me, and how His blood was shed for the remission of my sins, I felt something happening inside of me. At last someone had come and was showing me the way to find peace. I wept and wept. I believed what you said about Jesus. I didn't fully understand it but I believed it and I felt that my whole life was being transformed by a miracle.

I repeated your prayer as you directed us. Oh what peace came into my heart when I welcomed Jesus into my life. My mind and thoughts seemed to be washed clean. My heart was changed. I felt no guilt or shame before God. I felt I had recovered dignity. I was identified with Jesus. I had never had such peace and joy. I knew I was saved. I had a new life. I knew it was Jesus' life.

I threw away my religious robes and got some ordinary cloth to wear. I am changed forever.

Now the rest of my life shall be consecrated to telling others about Jesus Christ, God's Son who is my Savior. I am so happy.

That dear old woman went back to the village of her people to tell them about Jesus. It was not long before she was teaching groups of them about God's love and together, they built a bamboo and thatch meeting house which has since became a thriving church in that village.

You can experience the discovery of peace and dignity with God, while you are reading this book.

Bible References:

1. Ps.86:15
   Ps.111:4
2. Mt.9:36
   Mt.14:14
   Mt.18:27
   Mk.1:41
   Mk.6:34
3. Lam.3:22
4. Ps.86:5
5. Jer.32:41
6. Lu.9:56
   Na.1:7
7. Jl.2:26
   Ec.5:18-19
   Pr.10:22
   Ps.68:19
   Ps.104:24
   3Jn.2
8. Jn.10:10
9. Jn.3:17
10. 2Co.5:17
11. Nu.23:19 Moff.
12. Jn.3:16
13. Jn.3:18
14. Jn.3:36
15. 2Co.5:21 LB
16. 1Jn.4:9
17. 1Jn.4:10
18. 1S.2:8
    Ps.113:7-8
19. Ro.10:12-13

Dr. Daisy and her husband, T.L., share a commitment to help women everywhere to discover their value in Christ.

Zaire President's private helicopter carries his special guests, T.L. & Daisy, to visit interior areas of the nation.

Always teammates in God's work, Daisy and T.L. complement each other's ministries as they proclaim Christ to the masses.

IX

RECOGNIZE

YOUR

VALUE

AS YOU DISCOVER your value to yourself, to people, and to God, you will never cower or bow before another human person again. You will recognize the real *you* that God designed, and you will begin to practice the awareness of that new *you* by adjusting your habits, your lifestyle.

You will stand up, you will square your shoulders, you will lift your head and your eyes, because your worth has been fixed forever, by the price that God paid for you.

Discover five facts to trust, five miracle results, and seven steps to true identity.

Chapter 9

RECOGNIZE YOUR VALUE

THERE IS NO FACT of life that is as vital to your success and true happiness, as to distinguish your identity as a unique human person, created in the image of God, and destined by Him for significance and for productivity in this life.

You will never again cower or crawl or acquiesce or surrender or bow before another human person.

Rather, you will stand up, you will square your shoulders, you will lift your head and your eyes, you will walk with a sure stride.

Your Worth Is Fixed Forever

God proved how much He esteems you, by what He paid for you — the price of His Son. That fixes forever your worth.

You are ready to *Recognize Your Value* when you begin to esteem the real *you* that God designed, and when you begin to practice the awareness of that new *you* that came to be when you received Christ. As you learn to do that you will adjust your habits, your thoughts, your words, and your lifestyle accordingly.

This opens the gates to God's riches, to His health, to His success and to His blessings which He has provided so abundantly for YOU.

Confidence Is Vital

To understand why Jesus Christ came, and how to *Recognize Your Value* as His royal partner, you need to understand the problem that existed in the beginning.

God's plan was to reproduce Himself in Adam and in Eve, and to enjoy companionship with each of them.

He placed Adam and Eve in the garden of Eden and gave them *every tree that is pleasant to the eye and good for food; and the tree of life also in the midst of the garden.*[1]

God made one single restriction in order to measure their faith: *You may eat from every tree in the garden, except the tree of knowing good and evil; the day that you eat from it, you will certainly die.*[2]

God expects us to have confidence in what He said.

If Adam and Eve trusted in God's integrity, they would live and prosper with Him forever. If they abused His trust and disbelieved His word, the process of deterioration would begin and they would die. Their lack of trust was called *sin*.

The simple rule that God made was: *The person who sins will die.*[3]   Later it was repeated in another way: *The wages of sin is death.*[4]

Breached Relationship

God wanted the human persons whom He had created to have total happiness, divine purpose and abundant living.

Then Satan, God's enemy, heard of God's dream and conceived a scheme to induce Adam and Eve to betray God's trust.

He came into the garden, asserting himself as an authority and said: If you eat of that tree, *you will NOT die.*[5]

Eve was deceived.   Adam collaborated.   After Eve ate of the fruit, *She also gave to her husband WITH HER, and he ate.*[6]

Then God came and spelled out what the results would be:

There was no longer a basis for their relationship with God.   Adam and Eve had chosen to disbelieve what God had said.   They had breached their relationship with Him.

They were no longer qualified to dwell in the garden with God. Separated from His abundance and having forfeited His protection, they were now subject to their new *master*, Satan, whom they had chosen to believe.

Degeneration Began

That was the beginning of suffering, shame, disease, hate, lust, envy, murder, jealousy, loneliness, guilt, poverty, hunger, destruction and death.

Whereas, by one person sin entered into the world, and death by sin; so death passed upon all persons, for that all have sinned.[7]

The sin which abrogated the relationship between humankind and God, was the choice to disbelieve what God had said.

Deterioration set in like a terminal cancer. *The wages of sin is DEATH.*[8]

When you do not trust God, you do not trust yourself, or others. You die inside.

When you decide that God has no integrity, your own integrity is abandoned. Conscience becomes calloused. Dignity is deprecated. The human person deteriorates and dies. The light goes out. There is only darkness.

But *God is love.*[9] Love never quits.

Love Paid The Price

God's love went into action the day Adam and Eve sinned. He found a way to restore humankind back to Him. He would end the scourge of death and restore people to life. *Substitution* was the legal answer.

If someone who is innocent of sin would willingly take the place of one who is guilty, then the guilty one would be free and restored, as though no wrong had ever been done. That was love's idea.

God so loved the world that He gave His only begotten son, that whoever believes in Him should not perish but have everlasting life.[10]

In order to provide you a substitute who was without sin, God gave His own son.

Jesus was born by a miracle. The Spirit of God overshadowed a virgin and the seed of Divine Life was created in her womb. Jesus was not born of human seed, infected by sin.

Then God's Son had to be subjected to the same temptations of sin as any other individual. He had to prove that God's original plan could work — that people could choose God's word, rather than to dishonor God's integrity.

Jesus was tempted by Satan just as Adam and Eve had been tempted in the Garden of Eden. He was led into the wilderness where Satan came to Him, exactly as he had come to Adam and Eve.

But every time Satan brought question on God's word, Jesus asserted what God said.[11] He believed God's word.

The Bible says, He was in every respect tested as we are, yet without committing any sin.[12]

Jesus Christ was perfect.   He was un-touched by the seed of sin.

That explains why He was able to be your substitute.   Since He had no sin in Him, and since He had committed no sin of His own, He could assume for your sins and give His life as a ransom for you.

Since Jesus Christ suffered the penalty you deserved, and since He did it on your behalf, you are no longer guilty before God and you need never be judged for any sin you ever com-mitted.

No debt can be paid twice. No crime can be punished twice. So, if you can only believe, you are restored as though you had never sinned.

The judgment you deserved was put on Jesus Christ your substitute, in your place, and that judgment can never be imposed on you again.

This is the crux of God's salvation plan.

Basis For The Love Plan

God's plan is based on faith and trust in what He says.

Christ has brought you (back) *into the very presence of God, through His death on the cross, and you are* (now) *standing there before Him with nothing left against you ... the only condition is that you fully believe the Truth ... convinced of the good news that Jesus died for you, and never shifting from trusting Him ...* [13]

Now you have the right of choice. You are free to accept the validity of what Christ did on your behalf, or to reject it as superstition or as irrelevant or as insignificant.

Anyone who believes in Jesus Christ is not judged at all.[14]

All who trust God's Son to save them have eternal life.[15]

What specifically are you to *trust* or to *believe?*

I.

That Jesus was sinless and perfect;[16]

II.

That He died on YOUR behalf and that He bore the judgment which you should have borne;[17]

III.

That He did it because God loves you and wants to live with you;[18]

IV.

That God values you so much that He paid this infinite price to make that possible.[19]

You *Recognize Your Value* by believing those facts which constitute what is called the gospel or good news.

GOSPEL FACT 1.

Jesus suffered the penalty of your sins so that you can be saved from death and live eternally as He planned for you.

GOSPEL FACT 2.

He suffered the consequences of your sins so that you can be forever absolved from guilt, condemnation or judgment.

GOSPEL FACT 3.

He took upon Himself your pains, infirmities and sicknesses, so that you can be free of them and live in health and enjoy longevity.

GOSPEL FACT 4.

He bore your insecurity, shame, inferiority and loneliness, so that you can live in fellowship with God again.

GOSPEL FACT 5.

He died so that you can live.

GOSPEL FACT 6.

He assumed your guilt so that you can receive His righteousness.

Identity With Christ

God took the sinless Christ and poured into Him YOUR SINS. Then, in exchange, He pours GOD'S GOODNESS INTO YOU.[20]

All of your sins were charged to Christ's account. Then He assumed your guilt and bore the judgment which you deserved.

In exchange, Christ's righteousness was credited to your account and you were declared righteous in God's eyes, forever.

When you decide to identify with what Jesus Christ did, you will experience a miracle.

MIRACLE I.

The righteousness of Christ will be transferred to you and you will be free of all guilt and judgment.[21]

MIRACLE II.

Jesus Christ will come and live the life of God in and through you.[22]

MIRACLE III.

You will become a new creation.[23]

MIRACLE IV.

You will be restored to God according to His original plan.[24]

MIRACLE V.

A supernatural power will be given to you which will make you a child of God.[25] It will be a miracle.

Christ opened the way for God to come to you and for you to come to Him.

Blessings Through Believing

When you welcome Jesus Christ into your life by faith, there are several miraculous results which can take place in you because the Bible says, *Now is the accepted time; Now is the day of salvation.*[26] That promise is for you.

BLESSING I.

You are re-born, re-created, restored to God, made new. You become a child of God.

When you receive Jesus Christ, God gives you the miracle power to become His child.[27]

BLESSING II.

You receive a new spiritual life, the miracle life of God through Jesus Christ in you.

If you are in Christ, you are a new creature ... All things become new.[28]

Jesus said, I am come that you might have Life more abundantly.[29]

BLESSING III.

You receive total peace. Anxiety, hypertension, fear, guilt and condemnation are gone forever.

Jesus said, Peace I leave with you, My peace I give unto you.[30]

Being justified by faith, you have peace with God through your Lord Jesus Christ.[31]

BLESSING IV.

You are restored to friendship, fellowship and life with God — the way you were designed to live on this earth.

Truly your fellowship is with the Father, and with His Son Jesus Christ.[32]

God says, *I will dwell in them, and walk in them; and I will be a Father unto you, and you shall be My sons and My daughters.*[33]

BLESSING V.

Your physical body is affected so much by this new inner peace with God that your sicknesses disappear and you experience new physical and mental health.

You will serve the Lord your God, and He will take sickness away from the midst of you.[34]

The Lord forgives all of your iniquities; he heals all of your diseases.[35]

God's Way To New Life

In order to help YOU to *Recognize Your Value* and to receive God's life by accepting Jesus Christ, I will outline for you the way to be restored to God.

I.

Believe you are valuable, as God's creation.

For you are God's workmanship.[36]

God created male and female in His own image, in the likeness of God.[37]

You, Lord, have made people a little lower than the angels (Original Hebrew: *a little lower than God*), *and crowned them with glory and honor. The Lord has given them dominion over the works of His hands; He has put all things under their feet.*[38]

II.

Know that distrusting God's Word is the original and basic sin.

And the Lord told Adam and Eve, Of every tree of the garden you may freely eat; but of the tree of the knowledge of good and evil, you shall NOT EAT OF IT; for in the day that you eat of it YOU SHALL SURELY DIE.[39]

Satan tempted them to DISTRUST God's word by saying, *you will NOT surely die.*[40]

Eve took of the fruit and ATE IT, and gave some to her husband with her; and he ate it.[41]

That was the original sin — distrusting God's word.

III.

Understand that disavowing God's integrity results in death.

God said, in the day that you disobey instructions and eat the fruit I forbade, YOU WILL SURELY DIE.[42]

The wages of sin (disobeying the integrity of God's word) *IS DEATH.*[43]

Whereas, by one person sin entered into the world, and DEATH BY SIN; so death passed upon all persons, for that all have sinned.[44]

IV.

Believe that God valued you too much to let you die.

God was not willing that ANY should perish, but that all should come to repentance.[45]

God so loved the world that He gave His only begotten Son, that WHOEVER believes in Him will not perish, but have everlasting life.[46]

But God showed His great love for you by sending Christ to die for you.[47]

V.

Know why Jesus came and died as your substitute.

Since *the penalty of sin is death*,[48] and since *death passed upon all persons because ALL have sinned*,[49] all would have to die for their sins — unless a guiltless substitute would willingly pay our penalty by dying in our place.

Jesus Christ, God's Son was in all points tempted like as we are, yet without sin.[50] *He did no sin.*[51]

Being made perfect, Jesus Christ became the author of eternal salvation.[52]

Jesus Christ bare our sins in His own body, that we, being dead to sins, should live unto righteousness.[53]

God made Jesus Christ who knew no sin to be made sin on OUR behalf, so that in Him WE might share the righteousness (or life) *of God.*[54]

VI.

Identify with Christ's death, burial and resurrection.

A.   When Jesus Christ died, your old life of sin died with Him.   Identify with His death for you. *I have been crucified with Christ.*[55]

B.   When Jesus Christ was buried, your old life of sin was put away forever. Identify with His burial on your behalf. *We are buried with Jesus Christ into death.*[56]

C.   When Jesus Christ arose from the dead, you were raised up with Him.   Identify with His resurrection.   *God has raised Jesus Christ from the dead and has quickened you together with Him, having forgiven you all trespasses.*[57]

D.   When Jesus Christ arose in a new life, you arose to walk in that same new life of God. Identify with the new life of Christ. *Like as Christ was raised up from the dead by the glory of the Father, even so we also should walk in NEWNESS OF LIFE.*[58]   *You are risen with Christ.*[59]   *Christ is your life.*[60]

VII.

Believe the gospel and receive Jesus Christ in person now.

God's plan for you is based on faith in the integrity of His word and on your right to choose to believe it.

Believe on the Lord Jesus Christ and you will be saved.[61]

As many as receive Jesus Christ, He gives to them power to become the children of God.[62]

Relate or associate yourself with Jesus Christ because He is the way, the bridge, the link, the key that makes possible your reunion with God and God's reunion with you.

Now you can come home to God who created you and who values you.

Now God can come home to you and live in and through you, which was His original dream.

Right now, find a place alone with God. Pray this prayer, out loud.

O GOD, my Father in heaven:

It **was** You, who wonderfully created me, in Your own image and likeness. My life has great value.

I know I must never destroy what You created, nor despise what You love.

I now know that I am made to walk with You. I was never created for loneliness, sickness, inferiority or guilt.

I have disregarded Your integrity and this has separated me from Your life. All that remains is deterioration and death.

Now I know that Your dream was to live in me. Though I sinned, You found a way to save me from deterioration and death.

You gave Your Son, Jesus Christ to come to this world. He was tempted every way possible but He never sinned. He never distrusted Your word or denied Your integrity. He was perfect and without sin.

He became my substitute and assumed the punishment for all of my sins, when He died on the cross.

I do here and now, *Recognize My Value* by believing on Jesus Christ.

When He died, my old sinful life died.

When Jesus was buried, my old sinful life was buried.

When Jesus was raised up from the dead in a new life, His new life was offered to me.

I open my heart and receive Jesus Christ and His new LIFE in me now.

I do believe that You have now come back to live in me like You originally planned when You created me. You and I are one again.

LORD, since You paid the full price for my transgressions, there can never be any further price for me to pay. Now I am restored to God my Father.

All of the abundance You created on this earth is for my blessing. Now, You will supply everything I need, and guide me in obtaining it.

You are my Great Physician. Your miracle life is the healing life in me now.

There will be no more loneliness because You are my friend.

My sins are punished. They can never be punished AGAIN. My debt is paid. No debt can ever be paid TWICE. I am saved — here and now. I believe, and I am free.

Thank You Lord.

Amen.

Bible References:

1. Ge.2:9
2. Ge.2:16-17
3. Eze.18:4,20
4. Ro.6:23
5. Ge.3:4
6. Ge.3:6
7. Ro.5:12
8. Ro.6:23
9. 1Jn.4:8
10. Jn.3:16
11. Mt.4:1-11
12. He.4:15
13. Col.1:22-23 LB
14. Jn.3:18
15. Jn.3:36
16. 1Jn.3:5
    1Pe.2:22
    2Co.5:21
17. Isa.53:5,6
    Col.1:9-12LB
    Ro.5:8LB
    1Pe.2:24
    2Co.5:21
    Ro.8:1
18. Ro.5:11LB
    Col.2:10LB
    2Co.6:16,18
    1Jn.1:3

19. Jn.3:16
    1Jn.3:16
    2Pe.1:3
20. 2Co.5:21
21. Ro.5:11
    Ro.8:1
    Jn.5:24
22. 2Co.6:16
    Ep.2:22
    Ga.2:20
    Jn.14:23
23. 2Co.5:17
    Ez.11:19
    Ro.6:4
    Ga.6:15
    Ep.4:24
24. Col.3:10
    Ro.12:2
25. John 1:12
26. 2Co.6:2
27. Jn.1:12
28. 2Co.5:17
29. Jn.10:10
30. Jn.14:27
31. Ro.5:1
32. 1Jn.1:3
33. 2Co.6:16,18
34. Ex.23:25

35. Ps.103:3
36. Ep.2:10
37. Ge.1:27; 5:1-2
38. Ps.8:5-6
39. Ge.2:16-17
40. Ge.3:4
41. Ge.3:6
42. Ge.2:17
43. Ro.6:23
44. Ro.5:12
45. 2Pe.3:9
46. Jn.3:16
47. Ro.5:8
48. Ro.6:23
49. Ro.5:12
50. He.4:15
51. 2Co.5:21
52. He.5:9
53. 1Pe.2:24
54. 2Co.5:21
55. Ga.2:20
56. Ro.6:4
57. Col.2:12-13
58. Ro.6:4
59. Col.3:1
60. Col.3:4
61. Ac.16:31
62. Jn.1:12

At her International Women's Conference at the Osborns' world base church (Rev. LaDonna Osborn is the pastor), Dr. Daisy recounts the vision that she experienced wherein Jesus walked down toward her from a mountain of light, and said: "Daisy preach the gospel to women." (more next page.)

Dr. Daisy, with daughter, Pastor LaDonna, dedicates a large stockpile of life-changing audio and video Bible Courses, with manuals, on redemption truths.

Dr. Daisy assigns Bible Course sets to the delegates attending her World Conference at Tulsa from nations around the globe.

X

4 SECRETS

OF THE

JESUS LIFE

YOU WERE CONCEIVED and born with every abil-ity, every talent, every beautiful ingredient you will ever need in all of your life. Tap into your God-cre-ated uniqueness through the adventure of the Jesus-life.

God's ultimate dream for you is that you enjoy a golden lifestyle of happiness, success, health, pros-perity and plenty!

The extraordinary Jesus-life is the key to God's uplifting plan for you!

As you read, you will discover 4 vital secrets of the blessing-packed Jesus-life that I call the *New Life For Women.*

How can the unknown be an inspiration for you?

What is the irreversible law that can guarantee your success? Who determines your future?

What is the partnership link between humanity and divinity? Is it true that you are God's idea?

Discover the exciting answers to these probing questions and more as you read these *4 Secrets of the Jesus-Life.*

Chapter 10

4 SECRETS OF THE JESUS LIFE

SINCE YOU HAVE BEEN CHOSEN by God who has given you this new kind of life, and because of His deep love and concern for you, you should practice tenderhearted mercy and kindness to others. Don't worry about making a good impression. But be ready to suffer quietly and patiently.[1]

Be gentle and ready to forgive, never hold grudges. Remember, the Lord forgave you, so you must forgive others.[2]

Make the most of your chances to tell others the good news.[3]

And whatever you do or say, let it be as a representative of the Lord Jesus.[4]

In these scriptures we discover the beautiful formula for living the extraordinary Jesus-life, or what I call the *New Life For Women.*

Individual Opportunity

Why is this formula for the Jesus lifestyle so important for women?

Each person will give an account of herself or himself to God.[5]

Wives, husbands, your spouse is not going to answer to you. They cannot be blamed or credited with what you do or do not do. Children, your parents are not going to answer for you.

God looks at each person individually. And He has given to each of us the abilities necessary to live the exciting Jesus-life.

No Roles In Heaven

A good friend of mine once had a dream. She and her husband are pastors of a large and successful church in America. She dreamed that she had died and gone to heaven. At the entrance to heaven, she was asked her name. She said, *Oh, I am the wife of Rev. So-and-So.* There was no record of her under that name. My friend was stunned.

She awakened suddenly and began to pray, asking God about the meaning of the dream. He told her that her identity with Jesus Christ was in her own name — not in the name of her husband, or in the role of someone's wife.

This is a dynamic truth that every woman must understand.

You will answer for what you do with the life of Jesus Christ in you. You cannot use others as an excuse for being and doing less than what you are capable of. You cannot blame your spouse or your pastor or teacher or priest or bishop. You cannot blame contemporary teachings about *discipleship* or traditional interpretations of the *submission* of women.

Each person will give an account of herself or himself.[6]

And that is good news.

There are many secrets to living the truly powerful and productive Jesus-life. The four that I am sharing with you are essential and highly significant.

SECRET NO. 1
Say *Yes* To WHO You Are.
ACCEPT YOURSELF.

The Jesus-life at work in you begins with YOU and your acceptance of this fact: Wherever you were born, however you were born, into whatever family you were born, it was right. You were born when and where God wanted you to be born.

You Are God's Idea

I know that I am God's idea. I know that T.L. Osborn, my husband, is God's idea. I was the tenth of eleven children. T.L. was twelfth of thirteen children — born at Christmas time. Certainly we were not our parents' idea. But we are God's idea.

You are God's idea. You were born at the right time. Accept who you are. Never be ashamed of your family — of your origin — of your roots.

The liberating fact is, you do not have to stay where you were born. Accept your identity and grow from there.

I was born into dire poverty. My father was a drunkard. My mother was killed in a train-car collision when I was only 8 years old. Three of my brothers committed suicide. It seemed impossible to cope with the circumstances of my life. But when I accepted Jesus Christ into my life, I learned to accept myself — who I am. I love my family. But I have been reborn into a new family — God's family.

God chose your parents to be the channel to bring you to this earth. That is just your starting point. You do not have to stay there. You can grow from there.

Your Unique Self

When you accept yourself, then you can be yourself. Never try to be somebody else. Be you. You are a unique one-of-a-kind creation of God.

God's plan for your life is good. He has created in you the talents and the abilities to accomplish His good plan in your life.

When you decide to be yourself, you can willingly, cheerfully and beautifully fill the place that God has for you. That pleases Him because only you can fill that unique place.

Remember that God has as much variety as people will let Him express. You do not have to copy other people. That would be a tragic waste of your own God-created uniqueness.

God's View Through You

These exciting and esteem-building truths become reality as Jesus — living in you — is allowed to practice His lifestyle through you.

This is not spiritualizing a human truth. It is actualizing a spiritual truth. Truth must be applied to the need of human persons where they are, as they are. That is exactly what Jesus did when He lived on this earth. He introduced God's perspective into every day living. And now He continues that work on earth through you and through me.

Humanity And Divinity In Partnership

God is Spirit and those who worship Him must worship in spirit and truth.[7]

Truth is what I am sharing with you right now.

Truth is Jesus.

Truth is living the Jesus lifestyle.

Truth is knowledge.

Truth is Jesus living in you.

Truth is, that God is as human as you need Him to be; and you are as divine as God needs you to be.

Living the Jesus-life is a partnership between your humanity and God's divinity. The Jesus lifestyle is not all *spirit*. The spirit of God in you is the power that gives your ideas, your words and your action life. That is real *truth*.

True Greatness

True humility is accepting this fact: Jesus in you is as great as Jesus of Nazareth who walked this earth in the flesh. When you believe this and can say it without apologizing, that is power — power for living the life-producing Jesus lifestyle.

Never see anyone as being more important than you are.

God accepts you as you are ... but He expects you to become all He plans for you to be.

You Are In Control

You have the power to shut the door to negative ideas — to negative thoughts — to negative accusations — to negative fantasies. They will only give you negative results.

It does not matter how negative your outside circumstances are. YOU can be impenetrable. You do not have to be affected by negative people or negative seeds. When a negative word or circumstance comes at you, turn it around and look for the positive. Because for every negative there is a positive!

If you will look for the positive, you will find it. And then constructive ideas and new uplifting dreams will come to you that will elevate you, that will elevate humanity and will increase the Kingdom of God.

You are the only one who can open your heart and your mind to what is positive, to what is true, to what is good, to what is right, to what is constructive and to what is healthy. With the power of Jesus in you, you can go for it and achieve!

The Facts Are Good

Remember, when all of the facts about you are in, they are good.

Treat yourself good. You are the only self you will ever have.

Be yourself and work at becoming all that God has in His mind for you to be. That takes a lifetime. And that is what growing and becoming more like Christ is all about.

Work at growing yourself. Change can be positive and good. You do not have to be the same year after year. You can be a stronger, better person by living the dynamic Jesus-life.

This is not an admonition for you to change other people. You must accept others as they are, where they are — just as you must accept yourself as you are, where you are.

You cannot change other people. But you can change yourself — and thereby exercise a dramatic influence on others.

God's Great Love-Idea

Before Jesus came you were part of the fallen human race. You were separated from God because of the broken fellowship and the sin of Adam and Eve. Satan became the master, and all of humanity became the victim of his destructive goals.

But God loved you too much to leave you in that state. So He sent His only Son, Jesus, to pay the full penalty of your sin, and to bring you back from the dominion of Satan.

Now your life is new. You are forgiven. You are free to begin again — and to enjoy the beautiful fellowship and partnership of God.

When you ask Jesus to become the center of your life, your lifestyle changes for the better. It takes on new meaning. You can begin to live the peaceful and harmonious Jesus-life.

Jesus said, You are to be perfect, even as your Father in heaven is perfect.[8]

That is amazing. It is almost inconceivable that we could be perfect. Yet that is what Jesus said. So it must be an attainable goal!

BE perfect. That is a permanent state of being. Let the perfect Jesus *BE* alive in you — all the time.

You may not seem perfect today. But be aware that perfection is possible — and work toward it every day. Practice the presence of the perfect Jesus living in you. You will become more perfect, more and more like Him.

This is not the kind of perfectionist who has very low productivity. The perfection which Jesus is talking about is becoming like Him — living the Jesus lifestyle — allowing the perfect Jesus to live His life in and through you. That is a marvelous and productive way of living! Just think of it. When you begin to live the Jesus lifestyle, then from today you will constantly improve and be better, day by day, than you have ever been before.

Jesus died on the cross to redeem you. He willingly paid the price for your rescue. Now you have access to God again. And His plan for you is that you become like Jesus.

Jesus lived a perfect life as your example. Then He made a way for you to be perfect. Perfect in your mind. Perfect in your body. Perfect in you spirit. Perfect in your attitude. Perfect in your relationships.

His power in you makes it possible for you to live the Jesus lifestyle in this world.

Imitate Jesus

You will probably never be able to really accept yourself without a personal resolve to accept Jesus Christ. He is the one who paid to redeem you and who made it possible for you to

be the person God created you to be — a wonderful new creature in Christ Jesus.   Only
when you recognize what Christ has done for
you, and only as you accept Him as your redeemer and saviour — only then can you learn to
accept yourself as God designed you to be.

So, the number one priority for living the
Jesus lifestyle is — accept Jesus.   Believe that
He died in your place so that you can be truly
free.   Hook up with Him and become all that
God has in His mind for you to be.   Then you
can accept the wonderful new *you* that is created through receiving the Christ-life.

Rather than imitate others. whom you may
admire — imitate Jesus as your supreme role-
model.

When you ask Jesus to come into your life,
you become part of a new family. You do not
abandon your natural family. You just do not
worry about the negative things associated with
your natural seed.   You belong to the redeemed
family of God.   Jesus is the Lord of your life.
You can now live to the fullest — as God originally intended for you to live, by living the
Jesus lifestyle.

It is possible to become so much like Jesus
that everywhere you go, people see you as a
representative of the Lord Jesus Christ.

Be yourself.   Let Jesus live in you and express Himself through you daily — through your
thoughts, your attitudes, your words and your
actions. That is exercising the Jesus in you —

that is truly living the Jesus lifestyle — experiencing His uplifting *New Life For Women.*

Word Power

When you do that, you can say things like:

Greater is Jesus in me than Satan in the world.[9]

Those words are power when you say them with faith.

Jesus in you is greater than any obstacle you may ever come up against. He is greater than any circumstance surrounding you. Jesus in you is greater than Satan in any form.

You can say emphatically:

The Lord is the strength of my life.[10]

You do not say that you are weak, or incapable, or that you cannot do this or that. *I can't* is no longer in your vocabulary when you live the Jesus lifestyle.

You can do anything. You have unlimited ability. That is why you can attempt something new — perhaps more difficult than you have ever attempted even before. That is how you discover — *I CAN do all things through Christ who (lives in me and) strengthens me.*[11]

I exercise Jesus' unlimited ability in me every day. So when I find myself in a *dangerous* situation, this ability within me is practiced and

I am able to see the situation in its successful completion. That is living the Jesus lifestyle! That is *New Life For Women.*

You can say boldly:

The Lord is my light. The Lord is my salvation. Whom shall I fear?[12]

I am talking to you as a woman who has been around the world in many so-called *dangerous* situations. I challenge you as Jesus-woman or as a Jesus-man — in a dangerous situation, let Jesus use you to change the situation. There is no person or situation that need frighten you.

God Cares — Through You

God put it on my heart to go to Ghana to meet the head of state. At that time Ghana was in revolution. Jesus in me was not afraid. Jesus in me cared. And His caring always results in action.

You have to let go of fear in order to really live the Jesus lifestyle. You cannot be afraid of anyone or anything.

People told me all kinds of negative things about this Ghanaian head of state. I said, *I do not know anything about that. I just know that I have a message from God for him.*

By a miracle I was granted an audience with him, although the Ghanaian public had not seen him for five months. He arrived in the large room where I was waiting, flanked by armed guards. He himself was armed and carrying two radio telephones, with which he commanded his troops.

After I was introduced to him I said, *Sir, I have come today to tell you that I love you and that God loves you. He loved you so much that He gave His Son, Jesus, to die so that you can be saved. Jesus loved you so much that He gave His life on the cross for you. He cares about you.*

Best News Yet

Before our meeting ended that Head of State said: *Tell me more. This is the best news I have ever received.*

Never decide that anyone is closed to the good news of Jesus. Never judge people as being hard and unreachable. The world is searching. People want hope. Jesus is the answer. And it is a woman or man living the Jesus-life, who can share that good news with the world.

That great national leader thanked me for coming. He told me how he had come to the point of desperation. He wanted to help his country, his people. But he did not know what to do. He said, *Every day at 11 o'clock I come into this room and I meditate. I just open my mind to God and believe that He will give me some direction.*

He did not know Jesus, but before leaving I was able to pray with him and ask Jesus to come into his life. (Get our powerful book, *5*

Revelations for Your Own Miracle, and read the complete and thrilling account of this miraculous encounter.)

As you live the Jesus lifestyle, everywhere you go Jesus goes with you. All you have to do is discover the first secret for living the Jesus-life.

As you say *Yes!* to who you are — and as you accept yourself, then you are ready for —

SECRET NO. 2
ACCEPT GOD'S WILL
For Your Life

You may be asking: *How can I know what God's will is for my life?*

It is really wonderfully simple — perhaps too simple.   And you can discover it by reading the Gospels.

Simplicity Of God's Will

God's will for your life is that you accept Jesus Christ as Lord and Savior of your life so that you can be reborn into His family.   Then when Jesus comes into your life, He desires that you become His representative on this earth.

That, my dear friend, is God's will for you.   That encompasses everything that He is going to direct you to do.   And it is so simple that even a child can be a successful Jesus-person.

Practice wanting what God wants, for the same reason that He wants it. That is God's will for your life. And as you do this, your will actually becomes God's will expressed through you.

For it is God who puts it in your heart to do His will and then He helps you to do it.[13]

God's desire becomes your desire — and your desire becomes His desire.

You want people to be uplifted and happy.

You want people to be successful and at peace.

You want people to be healthy and active.

That is exactly what God wants! And that becomes your purpose as you live the Jesus lifestyle.

Your World Of Influence

Your family, your job, your community all represent your world of influence. It is your world that Jesus uses you to change — for the better.

Growing Power Is Going Power

You do not need to pray about whether it is God's will for you to go to China, or to India, or to Africa. Just be Jesus' representative in everything you say and do right now — where you are. Then see where you grow yourself to.

You may grow yourself to China as Jesus' representative there. And when you get there, you will be an effective, practiced Jesus-person.

A Good Decision

When my husband, T.L. Osborn, and I first went to India, we could not convince the people that Jesus Christ is the Son of God, risen from the dead and alive today. So we made one of the best decisions of our lives — we came back home to find the answer to the dilemma. We had seen the masses, our hearts were touched, and we had to know how to reach them.

We found the answer, and when we did, we grew ourselves back to India. (Get a copy of our exciting Classic Documentary, *The Gospel According to T.L. & Daisy*, and read the story of our search and our discovery.)

Jesus demonstrated the Father in everything that He did. Now He wants to show Himself in everything that you do.

That is why I can preach boldly and confidently that there is no difference between men and women when it comes to preaching the gospel and living the Jesus lifestyle. In studying the life of Jesus, I have discovered that every time Jesus did something for a man, He also did it for a woman. He was making a loud and significant statement.

Jesus showed us that God values women and men equally. There is *New Life For Women* the same as there is for men.

New Revelation

When T.L. and I were young people, no one had ever told us that God wanted to be reflected through people to other human beings.

This is a new revelation. It is the revelation that the world needs and wants and is going to have. It is in reality a revelation of Jesus Christ.

A Self-Check

The proof that you have the revelation of Jesus Christ will be shown in several ways:

1st: How you spend your time.

2nd: How you cultivate and develop your talents and abilities.

3rd: How and where you invest your money.

4th: How you treat other people.

Your Time

Time is valuable. It is more precious than money.

Time is life. Do not allow other people to control or waste your time.

How you use it determines everything else about your life.

Never *kill* time or *pass* the time. Manage it for your growth, and for the uplifting of others.

Your Ability

You are created with marvelous ability. You were conceived and born with absolutely every ability, every talent, every beautiful ingredient you will ever need in all of your life! How much of your talents and abilities have you tapped?

Remember, you *can do everything* because Christ lives in you. Attempt everything. Say *yes* to every opportunity that is for the betterment of humanity. Say *yes* to every opportunity for getting the gospel to people.

Think big — so that God can be a part of your thoughts.

Dream big — so that God can be a part of your dreams.

Build big — so that God can reach your entire community and your entire world of influence.

Your Money

The money that you earn represents your life, in the form of currency. How do you use it? Do you spend it on non-essentials, without thought or plan?

Your money is a powerful tool that enables you to improve your own life, and the lives of others.

Invest your money wisely. Plant it as seed in soil that will produce a harvest of plenty for you and for people.

Other People

Jesus made people feel important. When you live the Jesus lifestyle, you too will make people feel important.

You direct your desires, your concerns, your abilities, your money, your energy, your time and your priorities toward other people. And that is not selfless. It is your self, directed outward.

There is no such thing as living without people. When you live the Jesus lifestyle you are most assuredly a people person, not a hermit.

Since God is a God of love, you are a product of love. Your character is love. That is what you know how to do best. With Jesus in you, you do not know how to hate or to harm another person.

Since God is a God of forgiveness, you are a product of forgiveness. It is your nature to forgive, not to hold a grudge.

Since God is a God of health, you are a product of health. You are a direct reflection of His nature and character. You do not injure and diminish, but you heal and replenish.

God is the one who chose to work through human beings. He believes in you. He believes that you are good enough to do His work — of reaching and lifting people — with His power working through you. This is what I call *New Life For Women.*

As you say *Yes!* to who you are — as you accept yourself, and as you accept God's will for your life, then you are ready for —

SECRET NO. 3
ACCEPT The Principle
Of SOWING And REAPING

A principle is an irreversible law of God.

For example, there is the principle of gravity. When you throw a ball up in the air, it comes back down. You do not have to pray for it to come back down. That is because the law of gravity is in effect.

The principle of sowing and reaping is an irreversible law of God.

When I was a teenager that principle was held over my head like a rod. It was as if it applied only in the negative sense, and God was just waiting so that He could punish me for some misconduct.

I was 40 years old before I came to really discover that God loves me and that He is not looking for a reason to punish me.

God Is Not Mad

God is not mad at you.

He is not looking at your faults. He is looking beyond your faults. He is looking at the perfection that He created in you. He is reaching out to you constantly. You never have to be afraid of God.

This principle of sowing and reaping has become a very positive force in my life. Instead of fear I now have confidence because I see the positive fact of this principle — this law of God. There is no human power, no human authority that can stop the principle of sowing and reaping from working for you.

Sow good seeds. You will reap good deeds. Plan what you want to reap, and sow accordingly.

Realize that you sow more than just money. You are sowing or planting seed constantly with your thoughts, your words and your actions. Only you can determine the harvest that you will reap. Plant good seed.

Whatever any person sows, that shall she or he also reap.[14]

What Are Seeds?

Some of the most powerful seeds that we can plant are ideas.

Religion tries to disregard the riches of your mind. Your brain is your great communication center. Never bypass it. It is good. God gave it to you. Jesus redeemed it, and He lives in you to make your ideas beautiful for yourself, for His Kingdom and for people.

Research has shown that over 2,000 ideas go through your mind every day. That is almost incredible. What do you do with your ideas?

There are two kinds of people: Those who get ideas and do something with them, and those who get ideas and do nothing with them.

All of the ideas that you have may not be good. But sort out the positive ones and recognize their source. Simply get rid of the negative ones. Never accept negative ideas.

Not only are our ideas seeds, but equally potent are the seeds of our words and of our actions. When we plant them wisely, we guarantee our own harvest of good.

Multiplication Factor

In order to produce a harvest, seeds must be planted. If they are not planted, they wither and go back to dust.

Seeds cannot grow unless they are planted. Ideas cannot elevate humanity until they are put into motion. Words cannot lift another person unless they are spoken.

Seeds have multiplying power. You always reap more then you sow.

You can count the number of seeds in a piece of fruit. But who can count the volume of fruit in every seed?

It is the same with your thought-seeds. Guard your mind. Guard your thoughts. Guard your ideas. Guard your seeds. You are full of them. Have confidence in Jesus in you and plant them for the good of yourself, of the Kingdom of God and for the good of people.

You Determine Your Future

Your harvests of tomorrow are at work in the seeds you plant today. You determine your tomorrow — your future.

God planned it this way so that you can ensure your own harvest. No one can do it for you. And no one can hinder you. Plant the kind of seeds today that you want to reap tomorrow.

Your Friendly Future

When our 34-year old son died, I was left with a physical ache in my heart that I thought would never leave. It was there day and night. I prayed and said, *Lord will this ache ever leave?*

And the Lord said to me, *The one who can release the past is the one who has a future.*

This seed-idea began to grow in me and I have come to learn the importance of letting go — of hurts, of injuries, of injustices and even of the good times.

The only thing that you can take into your future from your past is the knowledge that you have gained from your experiences.

Your past is your teacher. Your present is your opportunity. Your future is your friend.

Never be afraid of your future. Secure it by planting good seed today.

Your good future begins by making a decision for Jesus Christ. When He hooks up to your seed planting ability, your future is indeed your friend.

You can trust seed power. Good seed always grows. You can bank on it. This is God's divine law at work in *New Life For Women,* the same way that it works in men.

As you say *Yes!* to who you are — as you accept yourself, and as you accept God's will for your life, then as you accept the principle of sowing and reaping, you are ready for —

SECRET NO. 4
ACCEPT Change

No one and nothing stays the same. You either increase or you decrease. You either live or you die. You think and stay healthy, or you think and get sick.

Everything changes. And that is good news when it is change for the better.

Revolution Is Good

Revolution, in the purest sense of the word, means change. Jesus was the greatest revolutionary who ever lived. Two thousand years after the arrival of Jesus Christ the world is still evolving and changing because of Him.

Look at the evolution of the worm which spins a cocoon and later breaks out of that cocoon to become a beautiful butterfly. What if the worm had been afraid of change? What if it had never spun the cocoon? It would have dried up and died and would never have known the wonder of being a butterfly.

Never be afraid of change. Evolve. Grow. Live.

The unknown is not a threat. It is something wonderful to be discovered by you. You will discover a world of ability in yourself as you discover the unknown.

When you come to Jesus and are born again, you are a whole world of new, fresh and dynamic possibility. Evolve. Grow. Increase. Become a better person. Live the Jesus lifestyle and become more and more like Jesus.

Look at a flower. First there is a seed. The seed is planted and out of it sprouts a shoot. Then a stalk is developed and leaves are formed. Next comes the amazing blossom. And after the blossom has matured, it becomes seed again. The flower keeps growing; reproducing itself in abundance.

Accept change. Grow with it. Reproduce in other people the Jesus lifestyle. They deserve to know about this *New Life For Women*.

A Self-Test

Check up on yourself. Are there areas in your life where you need to change?

What do you take into your mind? That is very important. That is where you control what you are going to plant and what you are going to reap.

What do you look at?

Who are your friends and associates?

Where do you go and what do you do for pleasure?

Never condemn yourself. Just examine yourself and decide where you need to change.

You can change by changing your mind. That is really the only thing in life that you can change — your mind.

That is repentance And you can repent — change your mind — about yourself, and see yourself as a redeemed child of God.

This is your golden opportunity to plant a good seed — yourself. Plant your life in Jesus. He will plant Himself in you. Give Jesus a chance. Give the good news a chance in your life. Give God's *New Life For Women* a chance to flourish in you.

Prayer

If you want to begin right now to experience this *New Life For Women,* pray this prayer right out loud.

Heavenly Father, in the name of Jesus, I come to You. Look on my heart. You know everything about me. You know every mistake I have ever made and yet You still love me. Thank You for giving me another chance.

I accept Your forgiveness right now. I repent of my sin. I change my mind. I turn my back on my old lifestyle.

I come to You, Jesus. And with all of my heart I plant myself in You. From today I promise to follow You. Plant Yourself in me. Lord Jesus.

I want to be a Jesus person. I want to live the Jesus-life. Today I say *YES* to who I am. I ACCEPT myself as a unique creation made in the image of God.

I ACCEPT Your will for my life. I believe that it is a beautiful plan that will make my world better.

I ACCEPT Your law of sowing and reaping. I will plant carefully, using this power that You have given me, to determine my future.

I ACCEPT change. I purpose to grow every day and to become more and more like You.

I want to love people like You love people. I want to lift people like You lift people.

Thank You, Father, for loving me. Thank you, Jesus, for living in me. From today I will live the beautiful Jesus-life which is Your ultimate dream for me.

Amen.

Bible References:

1. Col.3:12 LB
2. Col.3:13 LB
3. Col.4:5 LB
4. Col.3:17 LB
5. Ro. 14:12 LB
6. Ro. 14:12 LB
7. Jn. 4:24
8. Mt. 5:48 LB
9. 1Jn. 4:4
10. Ps. 27:1
11. Ph. 4:13
12. Ps. 27:1
13. Ph. 2:13 LB
14. Ga. 6:7